*"You see things; and you say. "Why?"
But I dream things that never were;
and I say. "Why not?"*

George Bernard Shaw

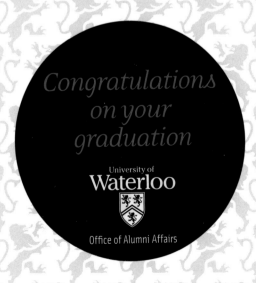

Congratulations
on your
graduation

UNIVERSITY of
Waterloo

Office of Alumni Affairs

University of
Waterloo

Message from the President

Ken McLaughlin has written a gem of a book. I read each chapter as it was first written, and it captured my attention like a good detective novel. I could not wait for the next chapter to arrive. The book celebrates 50 years of achievement and gives us a foundation for planning our next decade.

I received the complete manuscript in early January at the kick-off for our 50th anniversary year and read it on a trip to India over five days with Ontario Premier McGuinty's Trade Education and Research mission to that country. The two events are connected to this special book.

On the kick-off day, one of the special events was a reception for the elected representatives from our region. My message to them, which I had prepared the night before, was "the community made this university," and they and their predecessors are heroes and heroines in our cause. A few minutes before the reception I picked up our local newspaper, *The Record*, because I was told the lead editorial referred to our 50th anniversary. The headline of that editorial was "the university made this community." I remarked to our political leaders: The Record has its script, we have ours, and both are right. This is a symbiotic relationship going back 50 years. I was especially pleased that our 50th Anniversary celebrations singled out these elected leaders for recognition. It – like the editorial – emphasized how important wise and farseeing "political" leadership is in building both successful communities and successful universities and how dependent each is on the other.

The India trade mission was led by Ontario's Premier; he's also the province's Minister of Research and Innovation. The reason several university leaders were part of his mission is this: research, innovation and talented people are key ingredients for trade between nations. That idea is central to the University of Waterloo's Sixth Decade Plan, recently approved unanimously by our Senate and Board of Governors, which is entitled "Pursuing Global Excellence and Seizing Opportunities for Canada." My purpose in India was to extend the student exchanges and research collaborations with Indian higher education institutions which underlie successful trading relationships, thus helping to fulfill the precepts of the Plan.

The theme for our 50th Anniversary – "The Spirit of 'Why Not?'" – comes from George Bernard Shaw's lines, (paraphrased):

"Some people see things as they are and wonder why. We dream of things that ought to be and ask why not."

The first statement could fit many universities – the introspective questioning, energetic curiosity, unrelenting search for truth in its many, often unfolding, versions. In fact it is captured in the University's motto *Concordia Cum Veritate* – in harmony with truth. Wondering "why" is an essential piece of the higher education puzzle.

But the second statement is a signature for UW's history – first the dreams; then the value imperative of "ought to be," and finally the bold and daring "why not?" Ken McLaughlin's first history of the University, published for our 40th Anniversary, was entitled The Unconventional Founding of an Unconventional University. He returns to the unconventional theme ten years later with this book. But this is entitled Out of the Shadow of Orthodoxy. What is this orthodoxy we have left behind, and what is the clear light of day into which we have entered? The theme of our 50th Anniversary answers these questions.

In 50 short years Waterloo has achieved a level of distinctiveness more unusual than other universities. Distinctive universities are often characterized by four common elements:

A willingness to make choices, to focus

The foresight to identify strengths of the local community and to draw on, reinforce and extend them and make that community stronger, a form of barn building

The ability to project and trade beyond the immediate community and to be a beacon on a hill to illuminate a path for others

The opportunistic knack of drawing leadership from different and often unconventional domains

Ken McLaughlin's history, written around themes rather than chronology, beautifully and tastefully illustrated and rich with stories and their lessons, illustrates these four distinctive elements. Let me cite several of these:

The University's beginning can be traced to a challenge – Wanted: 150,000 Engineers – the headline of a feature in *The Globe and Mail* and the subject of a speech given by Ira Needles, the first chair of UW's board of governors, to the Kitchener Rotary Club in 1956. Engineering, our first faculty, was a local answer to a national and global problem.

Co-operative education, scarcely seen in North America, was shunned by established Engineering schools and made to work by industry employers who became trusted education partners – drawn right into the core of the university – and championed by the co-op coordinators themselves, all of them engineers who personally knew most of the employers from coast to coast. It is the most singular defining theme of UW.

UW's "creator owns it" intellectual property policy, unlike most others in North America, says we don't own your brains, we encourage you to use them to apply your ideas commercially and create both jobs and wealth for yourself and your community. You own the intellectual property that comes from your efforts, not your employer.

The creation of a campus landscape in which corn fields were turned into undulating clusters of cells for pedestrian interconnection, combining the ambience of the Harvard Yard and its quadrangles with the vegetarian patterns of Kew Gardens and Stourhead Lake in England, a setting designed by British engineer Mike Brookes and famous Harvard University landscape architect Hideo Sasaki.

UW's redefined physical landscape changed the landscape of the Information Age when after his return to England, Brookes, the university's first superintendent of buildings and grounds, alerted UW to the daunting proposal to put the Oxford English Dictionary online. Through the leadership of two curiosity-driven UW professors and hordes of undergraduate co-op students, it was done. The first paper version of the OED took four decades from 1857 to 1897 just to publish the letter A. The UW online version took less than four years and in doing so created the search engine prototype for Yahoo and Google and the local commercial company Open Text. In turn Open Text became one of the first two tenants in the north campus' Research & Technology Park, bringing industry right into the University.

A faculty of arts which grew out of rejection by Waterloo Lutheran College of a publicly funded university and then the imposition of religious faith requirements for faculty. From that rejection came UW's largest faculty establishing the comprehensive nature of the University.

The 'fearsome five academics' who defied the President and board chair's wishes, managed to get their vision of the purchase of a parcel of 185 acres of land, later extended by President Hagey to a 1000-acre campus, in place of the original, confining 20 and the clinching observation of two board members who expressed the sentiments that our successors in 50 years will never forgive us if we don't give them the chance to dream and grow. Dream and grow we have done!

The story of how a science and engineering school became a patron of the arts through an open thrust stage recommended by the early pioneers of the Stratford Theatre that became the centerpiece for theatre life for the Kitchener-Waterloo-Cambridge area for years to come.

McLaughlin's compelling narrative asks and answers several tough questions, while saving the toughest for last: why does one write a history book such as this? There are several answers. To understand and celebrate that 50 years of achievement for 50 years is a lifetime of experience. To understand the how and why behind the choices that were made and how they prepared the foundations for the choices to be made in the years ahead. To make those choices more wisely.

It is fitting that the alumni affairs office has arranged for enough copies of this stunning book to be printed so that each of the over 5000 graduates of our 50th year will have his or her own copy. Fitting because they are the stewards of this precious place in the next 50 years and will exercise that stewardship more wisely and more lovingly with the knowledge of what has happened to draw them here in the first place.

David L. Johnston

January 17, 2007

Bangalore, India

UNIVERSITY of
Waterloo

Foreword by Lois Claxton

The rush of excitement that comes alive in the story that Ken McLaughlin tells so compellingly in this book will resonate with all who know Waterloo. Unconventional, unorthodox, and, in the views of some, far too cocky, Waterloo has never aspired to conform. From its beginning, Waterloo's hallmark was to scale problems and cast solutions in its own individualistic way.

When I accepted Ken McLaughlin's invitation to write the foreword to his history: Waterloo: The Unconventional Founding of an Unconventional University, it was with no expectation that a similar invitation would be extended a decade later for his work that would celebrate UW's golden anniversary. But I find myself again honoured at the invitation and privileged to reflect on an institution that has become inextricably part of my personal and professional life.

When construction started in 1958 on what was to become the UW campus, my father began regular reconnaissance of the site. Assuming his young daughter would have as much interest in these developments as he did, we'd navigate the mud and monitor what was rising from the footings. And when a building came on stream, we'd take our own self-guided tour. I can well remember my father's wonderment at all that was happening.

What was happening was wondrous indeed but not inconsistent with Waterloo County's culture of initiative and enterprise. Long before entrepreneurship had entered the lexicon, it was flourishing in this county: in its tanneries, furniture factories, breweries, distilleries, tire plants, woolen mills, meat packing plants and insurance companies. The immigrant drive of the early English, Scots and Germans melded into a 'can do' force which saw opportunity and seized it. There was good reason why Waterloo County was enviably prosperous.

So when, in the mid-50s, there was critical need for more trained engineers in Canada, it might have been predicted that an unconventional response to this opportunity, a response which would result in the founding of UW, should be rooted in Waterloo County. A response proposed by business men who understood, though they would probably not have articulated it so, what risk and entrepreneurship were about. Core to the business enterprise and core to UW since its founding, entrepreneurship and risk-taking have been sustaining principles informing UW's initiatives across the academic spectrum of arts, science and technology.

The result is university which, having stepped out of the shadow of orthodoxy at the time it was founded, continues to be different, one with its own signature: where experiential learning is a defining feature; leaders of tomorrow are shaped; partnerships with all levels of government are consummated; fund-raising has reached a level unimaginable only a few years ago; and our reach exceeds our current grasp. Put another way: UW has the largest co-operative education program in the world; the Maclean's annual survey continues to rank UW first as producing the 'leaders of tomorrow'; the School of Architecture in Cambridge, the School of Pharmacy in Kitchener and the development of the R&T Park on the North Campus are all the result of unprecedented, partnerships with federal, provincial, regional and municipal governments; UW's current fundraising campaign which will close in 2007 appears likely to make it the most successful in Canadian universities on a per capita student raised; and over the next few years, as our 6th decade plan reflects, UW is committed to pursue global excellence by seizing opportunities for Canada

But if entrepreneurship and risk-taking have been at the core of this enterprise, so too has their ever-present companion: hard work. The roll-up-your-sleeves, get-it-done-now hard work. The breathless 'can do' hard work that arises from the excitement of seizing opportunity, setting new directions and crossing finishing lines first. We work hard, very hard. Ask anyone at Waterloo. Ask presidents and provosts. Ask professors and students. Ask alumni and donors. Ask custodians and electricians and groundskeepers. We work hard, but we don't work alone. Like the Waterloo county tradition of Mennonite barn-raising, the successes UW has realized have been the product of its people working together with commitment, with drive, with the collective will to achieve. People have made what UW has become.

What UW has become. Universities grapple with branding to get the concept just right. UW did too, at least Engineering students did when, in 1958, concerned that the world didn't know about UW Engineering, didn't know about Waterloo, in a midnight prank, three of them scaled the City of Waterloo water tower and painted BEER in bright red letters. Today UW doesn't have 'a brand.' It doesn't have to: say "Waterloo", and the world knows.

Waterloo. Who could have imagined so boldly where a spirit of 'why not?' would lead. Not I when I visited the site with my father some 50 years ago. Nor as a student here in the '60s. Nor when I came on staff in the late 70s. And on my frequent walks through the campus, like my father a half century ago, I gaze with wonderment at all that is happening. At the people who, like those before, are making it happen. People have made Waterloo. Waterloo is its people.

Lois Claxton, '68, Secretary of the Uninversity

Canadian Cataloguing in Publication Data

Photographic Credits

McLaughlin, Kenneth,

Out of the Shadow of Orthodoxy: Waterloo@ 50

ISBN 978-0-9682827-3-1

First Published in 2007

University of Waterloo

200 University Avenue West, Waterloo, Ontario, Canada N2L 3G1

On line orders through e-commerce may be made at: www.bookstore.uwaterloo.ca
or through the University of Waterloo Bookstore at 519-888-4567 extension 35444
or by e-mail: bookstore@bgl.uwaterloo.ca.

Design and Production: Bravada Communications Inc.

Printed in Canada by Friesens Corporation

Contemporary photographs of the University are by Bryn Gladding Photography.

Historical Photographs are from the Special Collections Department, Dana Porter
Library, University of Waterloo which in addition to the archival collection of
University images also houses the extensive Kitchener-Waterloo Record
Photographic Negative Collection. Other photographic images are from Graphics
Photo Imaging at the University of Waterloo or from private collections. We are
grateful to the Special Collections Department as well as to the University's Graphics
Photo Imaging for providing photographs for this publication. A detailed list of photo
credits and textual references in a printable format is available as a supplement to
this publication at the Special Collections Department, Dana Porter Library. The
cover images are by Bryn Gladding. All photographs are protected by copyright.
Copying of these images or text is strictly prohibited without the express permission
of the University of Waterloo.

TABLE OF
CONTENTS

OUT OF THE SHADOW OF ORTHODOXY
WATERLOO@50

Kenneth McLaughlin

Prologue

Waterloo is my university. At least, that's how I've always felt since the day in 1960 when I visited the campus as a high school student, gingerly making my way across the rough-hewn boardwalks and construction detritus, awash in a sea of mud, to an amphitheatre in the Physics and Mathematics building. It was a bright, clear autumn day in October and Don Trim borrowed his father's car as we left Preston High School on our adventure to the University of Waterloo. We were unsure of what to expect. If truth be told, we didn't know how to find the campus, but Waterloo is a small city, we thought – how could we get lost? We drove along what was then Dearborn Street, and at the intersection of Albert Street we found what we thought was a university campus. It was, but it was the wrong university. This was the campus of Waterloo Lutheran University. Its one ivy-covered building, Willison Hall, looked like what we imagined a university to be. Disappointed that this was not the University of Waterloo, we travelled further down Dearborn Street. There, where the road ended, was a muddy parking lot, some temporary wooden buildings, and a feeling of excitement that has remained with me to this day.

Waiting for us that first day was one of the most intimidating professors I have ever known. Keith Thomas, the Acting Dean of Arts, resplendent in a professorial tweed jacket and a flowing university professor's robe, bespeaking the medieval university traditions of Oxford and Cambridge, opened for us the wonders of civilization and the value of a university education. His manner was formal, his mien stern, and his vocabulary daunting. This day is as real to me now as it was then. Frightened, perhaps I was; excited, definitely; a sense of wonder and awe at the challenge of university life overcame me. Waterloo marked the opening of a whole new world.

There was no ivy on the buildings. There was no time for that. There was no doubt in my mind, however, that this was the place where I wanted to be. From the very first day, Waterloo was my university. Nearly 50 years later, the chance to write its history evokes feelings of excitement and challenge and admittedly some uncertainty, not so different from the anxieties I faced coming here as a high school

student. That these feelings have remained so strong over all these years speaks of the hold of the University of Waterloo on my imagination. Let me say from the beginning that this is no ordinary university nor is this a conventional history. Many university histories are formidable scholarly monographs, barely contained in two thick volumes, replete with administrative titles and scholarly ideas, following detailed sometimes mind-numbing chronologies. We felt that this was not appropriate for Waterloo. To be sure, archival citations, lists of professors, student leaders, sports victories, university administrators, Faculty histories and scholarly achievements are important and we have compiled much of this history on a separate website available in a printable format. This book is a contemporary history, as much about Waterloo@50 as it is about Waterloo in 1957.

Rather than a detailed continuous narrative, each chapter is a stand-alone essay that can be read separately and designed to accompany the rich photographic images of the University of Waterloo. Historical images are used sparingly and are presented in a separate signature following the book's epilogue.

Writing about the University of Waterloo over its first 50 years, I still see it through the eyes of a student as well as those of a professor of History. Like all students, I remember my favourite professors. Yves Zoltvany's passion for academic rigour and his excitement about revealing to us the mysteries of New France are part of my life. So, too, are Hugh MacKinnon's lectures on the marvels of medieval Europe, Paul Cornell's personal understanding of Canada beyond the boundaries of Ontario, and Father Norbert Lavigne's economics class where he taught the importance of "thinking outside of the box." Like many students, the friends I made then are my friends still: John English, Gail Cuthbert Brandt and I took European history together in an unfinished classroom in the Chemistry and Biology building and we are still in classrooms together, and still friends. I remember the frustration of other courses where I counted the minutes until classes or laboratories ended. Then there were the intense seminar discussions where I learned about the importance of give-and-take in university ideas and about the excitement of learning new ideas and bringing to class points of view that my professors had not considered. I think this is what caught my attention the most.

In the past, I have criticized the authors of other university histories for failing to capture the excitement of learning, which is so much a part of university life. Only when I came to write about it myself did I realize how elusive this topic is. For each of us the experience is personal and while this makes it no less real, it is difficult to generalize. Each experience of university is different, each is important, and each of us sees the university through our own eyes. We recall it from within our own memories. And that's as it should be. Not one, but many university histories could be written. I hope that the readers of this history agree.

I recall my favourite places on campus, the dances in the Seagram gymnasium and how nervous I was going there; I remember writing final examinations in that same gymnasium, and when I graduated it was also the Convocation Hall. In those days, there was no such place as the Bomb Shelter or "the bomber," nor was there a Federation Hall; there were no Tim Horton's outlets and pizza deliveries were a novelty. Student parties off campus were as common then as they are now, and they remain an important but elusive topic in university histories; sometimes best left unsaid, but very much a part of university life.

Sports teams are important in shaping the tradition of the University of Waterloo. Carl Totzke brought them with him when he came from Waterloo College. Basketball was played in the original Seagram gymnasium, hockey in the Waterloo Memorial Arena, (now the site of the prestigious Perimeter Institute for Theoretical Physics), and the raucous football games at Seagram Stadium, now University Stadium, created friendships and folklore. These, too, are important parts of the university's history. Waterloo was our university, and these events part of our tradition, even if our university was only three or four years old. Waterloo then was a small university and the players on our teams were also our classmates. This made sports events at Waterloo very personal, and when we defeated teams from Toronto, Queen's, or Western, we felt that Waterloo succeeded as a university. The other

universities would have to respect us. Many of us still feel that way about our university, and the other universities do respect us – but for this and many other reasons.

Had I captured all of this, I would have felt gratified and successful as an historian. Alas, many of these themes are not treated as fully as they deserve. I apologize for this. Other publications and other celebrations during the 50th anniversary, however, do much to rectify this, and in planning of the university's 50th anniversary, I was delighted to realize how many others share my passion for the history of the University of Waterloo.

THE BEGINNING

In the summer of 1955, Gerald Hagey, the President of Waterloo College, a small Lutheran-based Arts College in Waterloo, was worried that neither the needs of the college nor those of the community could be met without the addition of a science curriculum. The Lutheran church had been as generous as it could be with its financial support, but congregations were not expanding and most were in small-town Ontario and Nova Scotia. Lutherans in Canada had not embraced the university tradition as fully as for example, many Scottish Presbyterians, Anglicans, and Roman Catholics had done. Theirs was a more practical orientation. A majority of students coming to Waterloo College were non-Lutheran and, in the face of the college's very limited programs, many of Ontario's Lutherans attended universities other than Waterloo College. Change was inevitable for the college to succeed. A science curriculum would have to be added, and in light of the need for additional funding, it was entirely possible that the Lutheran Church's administrative control might have to be surrendered. President Hagey talked about this to W.J. Dunlop, Ontario's Minister of Education, and he also explained to Dr. Edward Hall, the President of the University of Western Ontario, with which Waterloo College was affiliated, that he "desired to participate in provincial grants to universities and colleges even if this meant an organizational separation of the theological seminary and Waterloo College and eventually placing Waterloo College under non-denominational control." Dr. Stanley Leavine, the Member of Parliament for Waterloo in the Ontario Legislature, suggested to Hagey that "Waterloo College might, if it was to receive provincial government assistance, have to obtain degree granting powers in its own right." These were the precedents that led to the founding of the University of Waterloo.

Hagey met with the Evangelical Lutheran Synod, and with their approval called a meeting of community leaders to gauge support for the development of a non-denominational science college to be associated with Waterloo College. The wording was interesting, for the new institution from which the University of Waterloo evolved was the Waterloo College Associate Faculties, although in the end it did not include Hagey's own Waterloo College. What followed is a fascinating story of personalities and intrigue, religious divisions and jealousies, disagreements and sacrifice, foresight and dedication, and fundamental differences of opinion resulting in two very different universities located along University Avenue in Waterloo. This story is told in Waterloo: the Unconventional Founding of an Unconventional University. This book, Out of the Shadow of Orthodoxy: Waterloo @ 50, is the sequel that takes the Waterloo story from 1957 to the present.

In the 1950s, universities were a novelty and fewer than five per cent of Ontario's students attended them. Only two Ontario universities were well known: the University of Toronto and the University of Western Ontario. Queen's had not yet risen to prominence and McMaster was still regarded as closely associated with its Baptist beginnings. The University of Ottawa was predominantly a French-speaking, Roman Catholic university and Carleton College, now a university, was a small struggling institution in cramped quarters in downtown Ottawa.

A new sense of excitement about universities, however, was also part of this era. 1957 was the year that the Russians launched Sputnik I and although the Cold War was not yet replaced by the space war, science and technology also took on a new importance in our national life. I vividly recall watching the satellite streak across the sky and students in the high school class ahead of me talking about taking evening courses in Russian at the University of Waterloo. How exciting it was. Waterloo was where I wanted to be. That same sense of excitement and social relevance remains integral to the story of the University of Waterloo in 2007 and is a dominating theme throughout its history.

The writing of this history was well underway in 2005 when I was invited to attend a retreat for university leaders at Kempenfelt Bay. This was a chance to supplement the archival records and the detailed files that had been the mainstay of my research. I sat at the table at Kempenfelt Bay, enthralled by the passionate debate about my university as deans and associate provosts examined Waterloo's successes and its difficulties, its international outreach, and the challenges it faced to become one of the world's great international universities. I recalled the archival files of President Hagey's struggles fifty years earlier when the university idea was just a dream. I thought, too, of how heartened he would have been by the

camaraderie among those who had committed themselves to the success of his university.

There is a popular photograph of President Hagey and his senior administrators at a large circular table in the first Board and Senate Room in the Engineering Building. I have often looked at this photograph and wondered about the people sitting there. In 2005 at the head of the table at Kempenfelt Bay, sat the Vice-President, Academic and Provost Amit Chakma who presided with élan and enthusiasm; for him, these were working sessions and he wanted to see his university rise to a new level of academic success. President David Johnston was seated to Chakma's right, arriving the previous evening with the battery for his BlackBerry discharged, but with exciting news from Queen's Park that for the first time in nearly two decades, the government had announced a major commitment to increase university funding. Johnston's enthusiasm, energy and his determination to see Waterloo succeed filled the room. Unlike the more formal photograph of university administrators during the Hagey administration, there is no seating plan at Kempenfelt Bay. In modern terms, the administration of Waterloo resembled a level playing field. To the left of the provost was John Bullen, from the university secretariat, who managed all of the detailed arrangements. Bullen was also a career civil servant at Waterloo, whom I had known as an undergraduate in the 1960s. Next was Adel Sedra, Dean of the Faculty of Engineering. The former Vice President and Provost of the University of Toronto, Adel Sedra came to Waterloo with the expressed intent of making our engineering faculty one of the

best in North America, recognized at an international level of excellence, and as he outlined proposals on behalf of the University of Waterloo, his range of administrative experience was clear. The deans of the other faculties – Ellsworth LeDrew, the Acting Dean of Environmental Studies, Robert Kerton of Arts, George Dixon of Science, Alan George, a former Vice President, Academic and Provost and the Dean of Mathematics until Thomas Coleman could arrive from Cornell University – kept a watchful eye and spoke decisively about initiatives in their faulties. Mike Sharratt, the Dean of Applied Health Sciences, was at his final meeting and Roger Mannell, newly appointed as Dean of AHS, was at his first meeting. Comments from the deans were rarely "territorial" and reflected the larger interests of the university.

In an earlier era, President Hagey had considerable difficulty in reigning in competing faculty deans who placed the interests of their faculty at the expense of the others. When President Pro-Tem Howard Petch replaced Hagey in 1969 he referred to the deans as "robber barons," and was shocked at the animosity he found among them. When he came as president in 1970, Burton Matthews faced down a revolt of the deans, and establishing the President's authority was one of his most difficult tasks. Matthews imposed a degree of order and administrative process on a university that was turbulent and unruly. He was so successful that when Douglas Wright, a former Dean of Engineering (1959-1966), replaced Matthews as the university's third president, he was delighted to see that Matthews' policies retained Waterloo's remarkable spirit of creativity. As the university's fourth president, James Downey maintained that sense of civility and commitment at Waterloo. There was no sense of rivalry at Kempenfelt Bay.

Opening the discussions, Associate Provost, Academic and Student Affairs Bruce Mitchell, presented a review of the Co-operative education programs at Waterloo. Everyone realized that Co-operative education had been an identifying feature of the University of Waterloo's first 50 years; now it was time to strengthen and renew it for the next half century. Catharine Scott, Associate Provost, Human Resources and Student Services, ensured that the interests of Waterloo students were equally as important as those presented by the Vice President, University Research Paul Guild, while the Dean of Graduate Studies, Ranjana Bird, identified plans to increase Waterloo's graduate enrolment and Gail Cuthbert Brandt as Associate Vice President, Academic stressed the need for Waterloo to actively recruit international students to take advantage of the university's programs and to add a breadth of interest to Waterloo's students, while Bob Truman verified and corrected statistical impressions of successes and failures of university initiatives. All this was carefully watched by Dennis Huber, the university's Vice President, Administration and Finance, and by Bud Walker, the Director of Business Operations, as they worried about balanced budgets and the need for new residence accommodation. Throughout it all, the Secretary of the University, Lois Claxton, retained a sense of the university's official memory and its direction. Somehow it was appropriate that Lois Claxton's voice recalled the university's tradition and experience. She was an early graduate of the University of Waterloo and her passion for the institution was evident. At the end of the two days, I realized there is another history of the university that needs to be written, one that cannot be found in documents alone, but written between the lines by those who strive on a daily basis to make this university successful.

The Waterloo story is one of adventure, innovation, excitement and relevance. A new university-can it really be fifty- caught my imagination that first day in 1960 and still does to-day. I hope that you agree. KMM

CHAPTER ONE

Out of The Shadow of Orthodoxy: Waterloo, 1957-2007

Each autumn the natural beauty of the land renews the feeling of wonder that is part of being a student at the University of Waterloo. The rhythm of nature reflects the changes in students' lives as the autumn colours, which symbolize the beginning of a new university term, are replaced by the rigours of winter. As the burble of the stream formed by Laurel Creek is diminished and ice forms along its banks, students' lives become more serious and mid-term tests lead to final term exams. Then spring arrives and the campus is reborn, as are students' dreams and hopes. Some leave for the summer break, while others in the Co-operative stream return for the spring term. For every student the experience of the campus is unique and personal. Everyone who has ever been here has personal memories of the special sense of place that is Waterloo. This is a university where students can play out their destinies, where the next vista always beckons, where the present meets the past and the future lies just beyond the next path. Waterloo is a university that touches the soul and inspires the spirit.

Visitors to the University of Waterloo today may find it difficult to imagine the turmoil that resulted from a Saturday afternoon's trek late in October 1957 when five faculty members, most of them newly arrived in Waterloo, donned their hiking boots to explore the muddy fields of a former Mennonite farm on the edge of the city's boundaries. With the crumbling foundation of a once-prominent bank barn, two empty silos, a large summer kitchen and smoke house, and a farmhouse where the last family to till the land had recently lived, it was not a prepossessing property. The faculty members stumbled across the remnants of an orchard, a small stream, and picturesque hillside, but mainly they saw an expanse of rough ground, broken fences, and tattered hedgerows. It was not exactly a university campus. No one thought of it as a place to build a university. It was to be an industrial park, and surveyors' stakes had been placed in the ground demarcating four acres where factories would be built.

Weary and exhausted, but also exhilarated by what they had seen and the dream they had of what might be, the five professors, Arthur Cowan, Ted Batke, Ralph Stanton, Bruce Kelley and Ron Bowman, sat down in the recreation room in Arthur Cowan's home at 237 Erb Street East to draft a letter to Waterloo College President Gerald

Hagey. Bruce Kelley, who had been at Waterloo College the longest, took the lead and Ted Batke, who had a flair for the dramatic, fine-tuned the words. No one knew what might happen next, but neither the City of Waterloo nor Waterloo College, the small fledgling Lutheran Arts College and Seminary in its midst, would ever be quite the same again.[1]

The "fearsome five" as they were later known, Cowan, Batke, Stanton, Kelley, and Bowman were the department heads of Physics, Chemical Engineering, Mathematics, Chemistry, and Applied Physics in the Waterloo College Associate Faculties. They had been recently appointed by President Hagey to a new committee – an Academic Advisory Committee – to set out the academic program and the curriculum for the applied sciences courses for the newly formed Waterloo College Associate Faculties.[2] All but Bruce Kelley, who had been at Waterloo College since 1947, had been recruited to Waterloo to help create a "science college," later revised to be a faculty of "applied science" to provide courses for arts and science students at Waterloo College. The plan was to expand the Waterloo (Lutheran) College campus by the Associate Faculties acquiring land along Dearborn Street (now University Avenue) toward King Street. Since arriving that summer, the "fearsome five" had watched with growing alarm as faltering campus expansion plans and building projections quickly unravelled, and as building plans overran the budget and local landowners sought to take advantage of the college's need to expand.

To meet the needs of its students that July in 1957, the first buildings of the Waterloo College Associate Faculties were two hurriedly-constructed temporary structures. Built by a local builder, H.E. Ratz Lumber, the buildings cost less than $50,000 and were located on the Waterloo College campus. They were on a narrow strip of land, for which the Associate Faculties paid Waterloo College nearly $30,000, located behind the old Willison Hall which housed the college residence, its library, and a gymnasium. Waterloo College's sponsorship of the Associate Faculties did not include either land or buildings. With so many new students in 1957, Waterloo College's campus was desperately overcrowded. Seventy-four students enrolled in July, and in the September admission ninety-six new students arrived

PETER RUSSELL ROCK

on campus. There was no sign that interest in the new Co-operative engineering program would lessen.

President Hagey, who was President of both Waterloo College and the Waterloo College Associate Faculties as well as a prominent member of the Lutheran community, wrote to Norman Schneider, the Member of Parliament in Ottawa, about acquiring the Canada Mortgage and Housing Corporation lands on the far side of Dearborn Street, but to no avail. Other negotiations for a six-acre property next to the campus boundaries, along Dearborn to King Street, where cows still grazed outside President Hagey's office, had also come to naught.

Attempts to purchase this adjoining property had gone from bad to worse. The Associate Faculties had offered $45,000; the owner believed it was worth twice that amount. The unsanitary conditions under which an adjacent property was being kept led the city health inspector to try to pressure the owner to sell it to the Associate Faculties. But the amount of land was of little consequence. Another major land owner, the proprietor of Swan Cleaners, with property fronting on King St., was prepared to sell his land to the Associate Faculties, but a financial incentive to relocate his business was a condition. President Hagey explained, "The only other location the owner will consider is the Snyder property on the south-east corner of King and Dearborn which would be available to the Associate Faculties, for a price of $36,000."[3] The total cost to the Associate Faculties, including the relocation of Swan Cleaners, was in excess of $100,000, and time was running out. As the summer progressed and no land had been acquired, a definite sense of urgency descended on the campus. Expropriation of these properties was always a possibility, but it was cumbersome and expensive and would not endear either Waterloo College or the Associate Faculties to the local community. Something had to be done.

In addition to the difficulties in acquiring land, the plans for a science building had also gone awry. Without the benefit of a specific site, the College's architects, Jenkins and Wright, developed preliminary plans

"In addition to the difficulties in acquiring land, the plans for a science building had also gone awry."

for a Science Building for the Associate Faculties, but the cost for the building alone was staggering. The estimate was $1 million for a structure approximately twice the size of Waterloo College's existing Arts Building. Excitement and a sense of uneasiness loomed at the prospect of such a large building and the creation of a campus that would be so different from the size and scale of Waterloo College. Some of the more traditional members of the faculty at the Lutheran College began to sound the alarm. It was all happening so quickly – too quickly, some were saying – while those in the Associate Faculties were beginning to believe that it was not happening at all and certainly not quickly enough.[4]

In the next estimate, the architects' proposal for the General Science Building increased to $1.5 million. The provincial government's total grant for the building was $500,000, and very little additional money was available from the local community. With a new sense of urgency, the Building Committee for the Associate Faculties met to discuss the whole problem afresh, hoping for a solution that would allow the board to proceed "with an adequate building, if possible within the original estimate."[5]

Complicating the problem with the Science Building was the architects' inability to design the Athletics Stadium and Gymnasium on Seagram Drive within budget. With a donation from the Seagram Corporation, the Associate Faculties agreed to build Seagram Stadium on land leased from the City of Waterloo.[6] Jenkins and Wright were now $92,000 over budget on the stadium, and a million dollars over budget on the science building: the Building Committee was right to be worried. Some on the campus had begun to refer to the architects as "Jenkins and Wrong;" others encouraged President Hagey to bring in new architects. Still, he hesitated. Jenkins and Wright were well respected and they had designed the College's Arts and Administration building, but Hagey was also worried about costs – and with good reason. The university might never be built. However impressive Jenkins and Wright's design, it was quite simply beyond the Associate Faculties' means. At the end of May 1957, the Board of Waterloo College Associate Faculties terminated its

agreement with Jenkins and Wright.[7] Now they had no building, no plans, and no architect. It was not an auspicious beginning.

With a building program gone awry, without land for the expanded campus and with no time, Hagey chose a Toronto architectural firm, Shore and Moffat, to aid in the design of the campus and the proposed science building. They had recently completed buildings for the universities of Saskatchewan and Toronto and seemed an inspired choice for the beleaguered president. Fate also intervened when the Faculty Advisory Committee suggested that instead of such a large general science building, they might instead construct a specialized Chemistry and Chemical Engineering building which could be done within the budget and in use by the fall of 1958. The decision against a "monumental" science building dramatically altered plans for the architectural style of the campus and created a new problem for President Hagey. As the committee began to set out the likely arrangement of other buildings, it became clear that a much larger campus was required than would be possible on the lands adjoining Waterloo College. A specialized Physics and Engineering Physics Building would be needed for the start of classes in September 1959. The following September, in 1960, a Mechanical Engineering Building, with one wing devoted to power laboratories for electrical engineering, would be required. In September 1961, a fourth building to house civil engineering laboratories and general engineering would be necessary, and by September 1962, if a science and applied science curriculum was to be offered, laboratories for sciences such as botany and geology would

have to be added. Popular support for universities in Ontario in the 1950s was optimistic and exhilarating; still, to consider establishing a university in small town Ontario was daunting. But that was the committee's mandate, and it did not hurt to dream of possibilities that were beyond the horizon.

Hagey persisted in his belief that the lands along Dearborn Street adjoining Waterloo College could be acquired and he instructed the architects to prepare a design for the "Waterloo College campus." The proposed Chemistry and Chemical Engineering building was to adopt the general style and brick tones of the Arts and Administration building. To avoid the cost of immediately purchasing property on Bricker Street, thus adding costs to the project, this grouping of buildings would be off of Dearborn Street, with the new building on the same axis as the Arts Building. For the overall campus, the lead architect, L.E. Shore, proposed a new Administration Building which would also include a theological school and a chapel that would be "in a dominant location off Dearborn Street and between the Arts and Engineering Buildings."[8] In this way, "the theological school and [a new Lutheran] chapel would dominate the campus from a central location." The symbolism of Lutheran predominance in Shore and Moffat's first depiction of the proposed campus is significant. It is Hagey's view of the university that he hoped to create around Waterloo College. It also represents a university that was not to be. The physical reality of six new science and engineering buildings created an orientation within the campus whereby the nineteenth-century conflict between science and religion

would be juxtaposed, threatening to lead inexorably to a clash of beliefs and interests. These early architectural plans suggested perhaps more than the architects intended and implicitly foreshadowed a debate that many, especially President Hagey, hoped to avoid.

On October 15, 1957 the Building Committee of the Associate Faculties submitted plans for the Chemistry and Chemical Engineering Building to the Board of Governors. With so little time to spare, the board approved the plans and recommended that the architects prepare specifications for tendering. If the building was to be occupied by September, 1958, it was critical to start as soon as possible. Problems with the previous architects had pushed back the schedule of the building program by at least six months. With the pace of college development increasing every day, six months was a long time to have delayed construction. As the new building was about to go to tender, finally, President Hagey thought his dream might still be possible.

THE CHALLENGE TO PRESIDENT HAGEY'S VISION

On October 29, President Hagey's senior Academic Advisory Committee called for a reconsideration of the decision to establish the campus of the Waterloo College Associate Faculties adjacent to the Waterloo College site.[9] The timing could not have been worse and their advice to relocate the campus was not what Hagey wanted to hear. He did his best to block their proposal. The committee's insistence that it be allowed to present its case to the Board of Governors of the Associate Faculties precipitated a major crisis. The committee had touched on a sore point. The shortage of land on the existing campus site and an earlier proposal to relocate Waterloo College to Kitchener had led to the resignation of Hagey's predecessor as President of Waterloo College.[10] Hagey, then a board member of Waterloo College, led the battle to stay on the Waterloo College site and subsequently left his position as National Advertising Manager for B.F. Goodrich (Canada) to become the President of Waterloo College. His hostility to the challenge by this group of newcomers was immediate and intense. Newcomers though they might have been, the draft of the memorandum was written primarily by Bruce Kelley, who had been at Waterloo College longer than Hagey. Although the others

may not have known the history of Waterloo College, they had a strong awareness of the requirements for a university campus and they doubted that one could be built "on the backyards of Bricker Street." They reminded Hagey that the campus of Waterloo College "envisages a maximum of 30 acres of which less than 20 acres are available for the expansion of the Associate Faculties."[11]

The committee came with a solution, pointing to the availability of a large tract of land nearby, within walking distance of Waterloo College, valued at $1,000 per acre. In an eloquent statement, they noted: "It is our opinion that if a University of Waterloo is to be built in the backyards of Waterloo College and adjoining houses, the citizens of Ontario, whose money is being used, will cite the project as a prime example of limited vision. The government, the Board of Governors, and the faculty will be jointly responsible for a patchwork of congestion in the heart of one of Ontario's most attractive regions ... If the views of this committee are found valid, then immediate steps are necessary to obtain a new site and arrange for the Chemistry Building to be erected on it by the Fall of 1958."[12]

When he read the committee's Memorandum, President Hagey was furious. While his public response was measured, in private meetings with committee members he was unable to suppress his anger, advising them that he had been making business decisions "when they were still in knee pants and that he did not appreciate their interference in the running of the university."[13] They were, after all, merely a committee to advise him. It was not their responsibility to involve themselves in areas of jurisdiction that belonged to the President and the Board of Governors.

He wanted desperately to avoid becoming embroiled in a campus relocation scheme. He recalled that an earlier attempt to move the campus to a larger site in the years following the return of veterans after the war had badly divided the local community. "Although the previous [campus] decision was made about six or seven years ago," Hagey reminded them, "there are still some people who are continuing to fight this battle, just as there are those in the United States who are continuing to fight the battle of the Civil War."[14] An interesting turn of phrase, this, and one that was perhaps prophetic.

"Without a full knowledge of the facts," Hagey explained, "it is easy to conclude that a mistake was made at that time. Factually, I think that history will indicate that the decision [to remain on the restrictive Waterloo College site] was in the best interest of the extension of higher education in this community." There was even more to it than this. Hagey believed that the committee may have had a separate and prejudicial agenda. He broached the topic carefully, outlining the moral and political support provided to the Associate Faculties by Waterloo College. "In reading your brief," he continued, "I sense that the suggestion to relocate involves more than your concern about the present site. Possibly my thoughts are unfounded, but I have the feeling that your Committee which exists between Waterloo College and the Associate Faculties [is] … concerned lest this relationship involves a handicap (financial or otherwise) for the Associate Faculties." Should there be such a concern, Hagey challenged, "I would think it would be desirable for it to be brought out into the open."

Rumours spread quickly. The idea for the location for the new campus was said to have been Les Emery's. Before taking a leave of absence from the Associate Faculties, Emery held the ponderous title of "Planning Engineer and Principal of the Applied Science Course" and was involved in a public disagreement with Hagey about the direction of the Applied Science faculty. Hagey distrusted Emery. "I assume that the brief has resulted from the discussion within your committee at its meeting with Mr. Emery this past Saturday afternoon [October 29]," Hagey challenged the members of the Academic Advisory Committee. "Should you wish to have your brief presented to the Board, I suggest that it should clearly indicate the individuals whose views it expresses. It should be stated clearly whether it is the view of your committee and Mr. Emery only or whether this subject has been discussed with the whole faculty and expresses the majority opinion of the faculty."[15] Now that it was out in the open, Hagey hoped that this whole proposal would go away. But that was not to be.

"Now that it was out in the open, Hagey hoped that this whole proposal would go away. But that was not to be."

CHOOSING A NEW CAMPUS

The Academic Advisory Committee persisted in their request to be present at the next meeting of the Board of Governors, but before doing so they met with the faculty of Waterloo College who also expressed an interest in the proposal. When Hagey agreed that the Board of Governors would review their suggestions at its next meeting, the committee members were pleased, but not overly optimistic about their chances of success. Although they would not be permitted to speak at the meeting, their letter would be included as part of the Board's agenda.

When the Board assembled on November 12, 1957, the Chair of the Board, Ira Needles, President of B.F. Goodrich (Canada), gruff and plain spoken, friend and mentor to Gerry Hagey, was unfailingly polite, but unimpressed and unsympathetic to the proposal. Hagey, himself, was taciturn. The members of the Board had all been chosen by him and by Needles, and he knew he had their support. So did the members of the Academic Advisory Committee who believed their ideas were destined to fail, but each time the discussion seemed about to end, one board member, Carl Pollock, kept it alive, or as Arthur Cowan phrased it, "Pollock kept knifing in."[16] Although a friend of both Hagey and Needles, Pollock was not a typical industrialist, and his company, Dominion Electrohome Industries, was one of the largest employers in Kitchener and Waterloo. A graduate of the University of Toronto and Oxford University, Carl Pollock was one of the youngest board members, and he had a keen interest in universities and a strong sense of what was involved in university life. Pollock's lone support, however, was not enough. The Academic Advisory Committee members began to worry. Was Pollock their only ally? By about five o'clock in the evening, Ralph Stanton looked over at Ted Batke and as he recalls it, "We both…well, in our eyes we said, 'We've tried, it's a failure!'"[17] Then, one sentence was heard throughout the room, as another lone voice said, "I think we should acquire some land right away."[18] A. R. Kaufman had spoken. Arthur Cowan remembers, "A.R. [was] sitting there, obviously listening very carefully with his wing collar…sitting there almost majestically…very, very proper…finally A.R. cleared his throat. There was a deathly silence in the room. In those days it was said A.R. owned a third of Kitchener." "I can't remember the words exactly," Cowan explained, "but it was something like, 'Gentlemen: I think looking back 30 years from now, we would be considered to be very small-minded if we did not look into this matter. I'll have my realtor look at it in the morning.' [Then the votes were] Yes, yes, yes, yes – unbelievable."[19] The Board agreed that Mr. Kaufman's real estate agent would look at the property recommended by the Academic Advisory Committee and report back.[20]

No decision had been made, but the land purchase had not been rejected out of hand. In the meantime, the Board recommended that the Chemistry and Chemical Engineering Building continue to be located on the existing Waterloo College campus.[21] More than just a new campus was at stake. Next, the board empowered the Academic Advisory Committee "to study the possibilities of this institution [Waterloo College Associate Faculties] procuring a degree-granting charter" and full university status. As much as a new campus, this decision would fundamentally alter the relationship between Waterloo College and the fledgling Waterloo College Associate Faculties. Meanwhile, negotiations for the purchase of land for a new campus continued at a hurried pace. The Management Committee received a formal offer from Major Holdings to sell the parcel of land west of the existing Waterloo College campus that had comprised the former Schweitzer farm. The committee worked tirelessly to review the proposal and to negotiate terms that would ensure both probity and frugality as such an important land transaction would attract considerable public attention. The offer expired on December 31, 1957. At a meeting on December 3, the committee worried that there had not been enough time to conduct a proper study of their options.[22] Nevertheless, with time running out, and the meeting with the Board set for January 9, a decision had to be made. On December 30 a new offer from Abram Wiebe at Major Holdings was dispatched to President Hagey. The Board of Governors was called into session on January 9, 1958.

President Hagey hesitated. He remained uncertain. He preferred the lands near Waterloo College and he wanted recognition of the important leadership role that Waterloo College had provided and of the obligations owed to the Lutheran College by the Associate Faculties. But, in reality, the debate was over. The hope of these lands and of Hagey's original plan faded when the city assessor indicated that the minimum cost of the land for the Waterloo College site would be between $300,000 and $400,000. To develop a campus on the land on the opposite side of Dearborn, Hagey's other option, would cost between one and two million dollars. Furthermore, A.R. Kaufman's real estate advisor had recommended purchasing the former Schweitzer farm lands. Kaufman's role was crucial: his moral suasion and the overwhelming economic and social influence he wielded in the community had carried the Board at its November meeting. His affirmation sealed the land purchase.

Major Holdings' offer was appealing. The land provided the possibility of developing a campus on the scale of other major Canadian universities. The terms of the purchase agreement were designed so the Associate Faculties would obtain access to the entire tract of land while paying for only a 50-acre portion in the first year. The purchase price of $344,240.50 for the total 183 acres was significantly less than the amount necessary to develop the restrictive Waterloo College rectangle. An initial payment of $100,000 made by January 15 would confirm the deal, and the Associate Faculties could pay the rest of the balance over the next four years. Additionally, Major Holdings would donate $25,000 to the Capital Account of the College in five equal payments over the next five years.

Before the final vote on the land acquisition was held, Hagey once again spoke emotionally to the Board about the Associate Faculties' moral obligations to Waterloo College, urging that "factors outlined in his report merited consideration previous to a decision for the Associate Faculties to relocate."[23] His intense commitment to Waterloo College jumps off of every line of the meeting's minutes, but no further discussion of the matter was recorded. These were businessmen. The deal was done. A.R. Kaufman, seconded by Preston industrialist Percy Hilborn, moved that the president's report be accepted and that "he be authorized to convey to the Waterloo College Board this Board's acceptance of the principles stated in his report." At last it was Carl Pollock's turn as he moved that "Mr. Kaufman, with the Administration, be authorized to negotiate an approved agreement with Major Holdings Limited and, subject to the approval of the Waterloo College Board, commit this Board to the purchase of one hundred and eighty-three acres of land as outlined above."[24] And that was it. The motion carried unanimously. The meeting was adjourned. It was not Gerry Hagey or even Ira Needles, but rather A.R. Kaufman and Carl Pollock, two of the community's most prominent business leaders, who had led the way. Pollock continued to take a strong interest in the University, in turn becoming Chair of its Board of Governors and ultimately its Chancellor. As a leading Canadian businessman and a president of the Canadian Manufacturers' Association, Carl Pollock took great pride in presenting the case to the Ontario government for this new university in Waterloo.

Despite the euphoria surrounding the land purchase, Hagey remained concerned about the impact on Waterloo College. In words that would be prophetic in ways he could not have anticipated, he forecast that "the decision for or against moving to a new site has possibilities of exerting an influence much beyond that of making possible a picturesque or scenic campus for a future university."[25] The following week, Hagey presented the proposal to a joint board committee of Waterloo College and the Associate Faculties. Starting a new university was one thing; somehow holding these disparate interests in tandem on separate campuses would be quite another and the struggle was not over. There was also the Evangelical Lutheran Synod to consider, for the Synod, not the Board of Governors, was the controlling power at Waterloo College and the Synod's denominational interests differed from those of the Associate Faculties. It is not surprising that Hagey feared moving to a new campus. Emotions always run high on issues such as these.

Not everyone at Waterloo College shared Hagey's commitment to creating a new university, and especially not one based on the Associate Faculties. Some continued to prefer the cosy relationship that had existed since 1925 between Waterloo College and the University of Western Ontario, whereby students at Waterloo College received their degrees from Western. This opposition would not be easily silenced. As a graduate of Waterloo College's Arts Faculty, Hagey felt passionately about the college which had done so much to shape his own life. He especially wanted to be reassured that the relocation to the new campus would not adversely affect Waterloo College, and that the Arts Faculty of the proposed university, and Arts more generally, would have an equal voice with that of Science in establishing future academic policies. Furthermore, Hagey also wanted to ensure that Waterloo College would be the dominant Church college in the new university, even though, as he put it, "[T]here was good reason to believe that Churches other than the Lutheran Church will wish to become associated with the University of Waterloo."[26] In light of this, he suggested it would be appropriate to recognize the symbolic and historical role of the Lutheran Church by reserving the natural knoll, the highest point on the future campus site, for a Lutheran chapel, "if Waterloo College wished to construct one." Earlier, he had hoped that the Lutheran Church might provide a chapel on the Waterloo College campus, "through which Christian services might be made available to students of all denominations." This was a possibility on the new campus and the Lutheran presence could still be a dominant feature.

The plan for a larger campus and the creation of a new university moved forward on January 16, when the joint board committee of the Associate Faculties and Waterloo College met to gain the approval for the land purchase from the Waterloo College Board of Governors. On January 22, Reverend A.J. Baetz, secretary of the Board of the Evangelical Lutheran Seminary, wrote to the pastors of the Canada and Nova Scotia Synods of the Lutheran Church that sponsored Waterloo College to explain the recent events relating to the college and the seminary and to provide them with "accurate information" as to the board's action before it was reported in the Canadian media. Of particular interest, he said, was the unanimous recommendation, "That the Board of Governors of the Evangelical Lutheran Seminary of Canada go on record as being in favour of relocating our Arts College on a campus mutually acceptable to the Board of Governors of Waterloo College Associate Faculties and the Evangelical Lutheran Seminary of Canada."[27] A joint Campus Planning Committee, which included the president of the college as an ex officio member, was established. Its priority was to determine "definite sites being assigned to Waterloo College for the erection of

its buildings" on the new campus. Hagey's fears seemed to have been for naught. His plans and dreams took on a new reality. It was more than he could have hoped for.

This major commitment by the College Board indicated the Lutheran Church still stood firmly behind President Hagey. Pastor Baetz explained that there were distinct advantages in the seminary having a location physically separate from the future university, just as there was "much to be gained by our Church College in being territorially closely related to the [educational] facilities provided to the university through government grants."[28] The relocation of the Arts College, he suggested, also "opens up the possibility for the expansion of our Seminary on its present site."

Three days later, on January 25, 1958, the story of the new campus and the likelihood of Waterloo acquiring its own university became front-page news in the *Kitchener-Waterloo Record*. The paper described the new 200-acre campus as "a major step in the institution's march towards its goal of becoming a degree granting university."[29]

It was all so incredibly positive. The land for a new campus had been purchased. The Board of Governors had instructed Hagey to seek university status. Waterloo College's Lutheran leaders had agreed to move the Arts College to the new campus where they would be able to choose a site that would represent their place of importance in the new university. Hagey immediately instructed Shore and Moffat to locate the Chemistry and Chemical Engineering building on the former Schweitzer farm lands rather than on the Waterloo College campus. It was imperative that the building be open for the September 1958 class, but it would be difficult to create a new building on a site that was yet to be determined and to install the apparatus for scientific experiments in eight months. This became the pace of development at Waterloo as building after building, with never quite enough time, seemed to be needed to meet the arrival of students eager to attend this new and untried university experiment.[30] With the final decision made and the building program under control, Hagey announced a campus plan that foresaw 19 buildings in the next seven years at a cost of $35 million.[31]

THE CAMPUS PLAN

The Schweitzer farm made a good choice for a university campus. Virtually empty farmland, it presented few obstacles to planning. Those elements that did offer minor challenges were natural features like the prominent knoll slightly south-east of the geographical centre of the property, an undulating landscape, and the small meandering Laurel Creek, which cut off about a quarter of the property to the west. The few structures atop the knoll comprised a farmhouse with two old and crumbling silos and the foundation of a barn near by. The CNR spur line to the east was the only pre-existing developed boundary; Westmount Road to the west, which curved around the north part of the creek, and Columbia Street to the north were dirt roads without municipal services. The impact of the University of Waterloo would be profound as roads and subdivisions soon came to surround its campus, but few will recall just how fundamental were the changes. The attractive boulevards that circle the larger campus, University Avenue, and Westmount Road, as well as Columbia Street, which divides the North and South campuses, which add so much to the character and beauty of the City of Waterloo, were created directly in response to the existence of the University and were built, in part, on lands provided by the University. The University also acquired several additional properties to complete its access to the Schweitzer farm and to the nearby Seagram Stadium. The development of a major Ontario university, where previously there had been cornfields, soon began in earnest.

Only Dearborn Street, which was renamed University Avenue early in 1962, offered a serious complication to planners. Like Westmont and Columbia, Dearborn remained a dirt road, but unlike the other two, it was to extend through the southern part of the campus dividing the land in such a way as to prevent a unified campus from emerging. Of the buildings currently on the South Campus, half of the engineering buildings, all of the arts buildings, and half of Dana Porter Library and Needles Hall would have been south of University Avenue. There was no time for debate. Construction was to start immediately on the Chemistry and Chemical Engineering building, located off of the original lane near the existing Mennonite

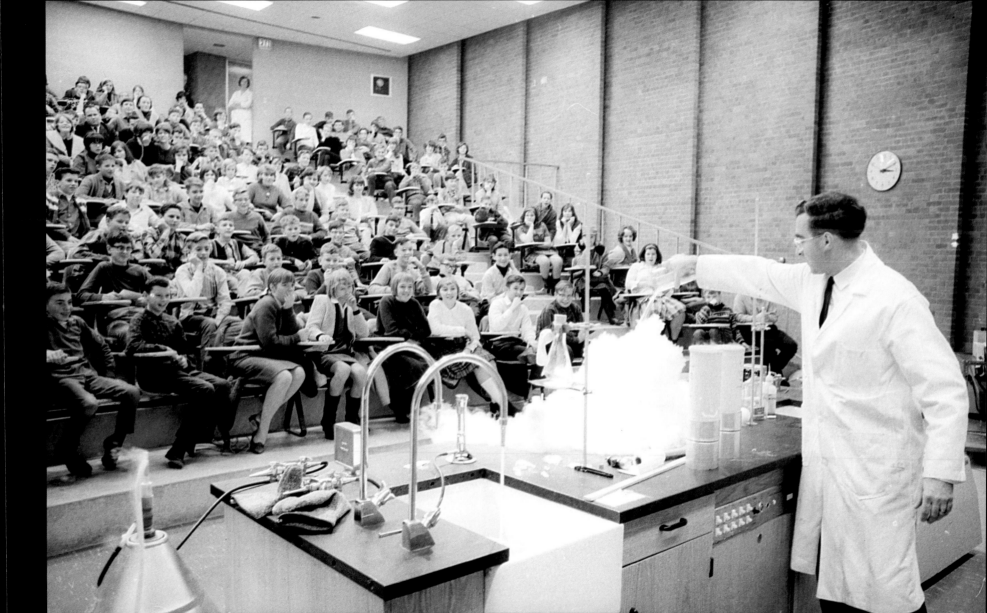

farm-house. The Associate Faculties sought to stop Dearborn Street from bisecting the campus. First, they requested that the City of Waterloo terminate Dearborn at the edge of the campus. (The remnants of this original road pattern may still be seen near the University Plaza.) Failing this, they asked the City to divert the road totally around the campus lands, but this, too was not to be. The compromise was to direct Dearborn Street southwest at an angle, dividing about 35 acres of land from the main part of the property. (While this was not ideal, in the long term it provided a solution to the problem of parking adjacent to the campus, with parking lots hidden from view by berms and attractive landscaping.) In the beginning however, in order to integrate the campus of Waterloo College and that of the Associate Faculties, the plan was to build student residences in this section. With Seagram Stadium so close, a series of student playing fields were also set out for this area of the campus.

The location of the Chemistry and Chemical Engineering Building in the southeast corner of the property, near the farm lane approaching the former Schweitzer farm-house, set the position of related university buildings even before a campus plan had been created. In part, this site had been chosen because the contours of the land resembled those of Waterloo College, and therefore, the already-designed building could be directly set into place on the new campus. The location was also proximate to the existing sewer connection and by situating the building with its "back" to the railway tracks, the intrusion of the rail line could be minimized. Think about it for a moment. This is hardly the ideal location for the first building of a university-in-the-making, and its architectural style is less dramatic than many had anticipated, but with so little time to spare, neither the design of the building nor its location were selected to impress. It's hard to imagine creating a university this way. Where is the grand entrance to the campus, its tree lined boulevard leading to monumental stone clad buildings, collegiate gothic in style, inspiring students and visitors alike with architectural references to great universities of the past? Not here, not at our Waterloo!

THE BROOKES YEARS

Hagey was undoubtedly concerned about how to develop his new campus, but in January 1958 he had other pressing matters, including whether students attending Waterloo College Associate Faculties would have their credits recognized for a university degree and whether universities like Queen's, Western, and Toronto would succeed in derailing the Associate Faculties' unconventional Co-operative education program.[32] These universities strenuously objected to Waterloo's engineering program and tried to have the Minister of Education block it. With all this and more on his agenda, Hagey gave responsibility for developing the physical aspects of the campus to Alan Adlington, who had come from a career in industry with Electrohome to join him at Waterloo College. His first job title was Bursar, but he was, in effect, Vice-President of Finance and Development. Adlington assumed responsibility for the financing of the university and the day to day management of the campus and he liked the play of large ideas and had a good sense of what a university might be. In May 1958, Adlington and Hagey recruited E.M. Brookes to be Superintendent of Buildings and Grounds (SOB-G). If ever there was an inspired choice, this was it. Brookes arrived at Waterloo with a broad range of experience as a designing engineer for projects in concrete and steel, and as a divisional surveyor in Durham, England responsible for budgets, programming, planning, and maintenance of roads, bridges, and buildings. His experience in researching and applying pre-stressed concrete in construction was a perfect fit for the University of Waterloo, which sought to use this building method to speed up the construction of its buildings.

Brookes recalled one of his earliest tasks entered into the lore of university history when President Hagey insisted that Brookes move the Associate Faculties' "temporary" buildings from the Waterloo College campus to the former Schweitzer farm in time for the arrival of students in September 1958. He arranged to have them hauled by Cooper Wrecking down the few blocks of Dearborn Street. It must have been quite a sight, as these large buildings were trucked to the new campus where foundations had hurriedly been put in place. One of the buildings was too large to move as a single piece and had to be

cut in half. The other building, slightly wider, became wedged part way along the street and was left there over night until, by removing the eaves trough and facia boards, it was moved forward the next morning. The mud-strewn campus – boardwalks, construction hoarding, mud, and more mud – had an undeniable air of excitement. As the Chemistry and Chemical Engineering Building was not finished, the "temporary" buildings or "Annex" were the centre of student life at Waterloo. One other building located off campus, nicknamed an "Annex" to the University of Waterloo, also had a fond place in the students' affection. This was the Waterloo Hotel, which the students had claimed as their own. In an allusion to the practice at Waterloo College to adjourn classes for "Chapel" each

morning, the engineering students could be heard to say that their "chapel" was scheduled for the Waterloo Hotel on Friday afternoons.

Mike Brookes's creative spirit and his love of the land left an indelible imprint on the campus. The University of Waterloo became a very personal statement of what was best in the university tradition and of the beauty of the Waterloo County landscape. Brookes set out to build a campus that would separate Waterloo from so many of the "new" post-war universities as he worked in concert with Shore and Moffat and with the Harvard University landscape architect Hideo Sasaki, whose ideas for university development shaped campuses across North America.[33]

With Brookes now devoted full time to Buildings and Grounds, the campus planning process was begun. With so many new buildings, campus development quickly outpaced planning. As the outline for the second building, Physics and Mathematics, fell into place, the problems of building location, timing, requirements, and costs made it clear that the university needed to quickly develop a larger campus plan. Previous attempts were preliminary explorative thinking, based on early ideas and theories. Shore and Moffat's report of July 22, 1958 established the university's planning for most of the next half century. Other architects would add new buildings, shaping the look of the campus, but none would have the influence of Shore and Moffat.

The guiding idea behind the University's planning was for a growth pattern that permitted an extension of the initial campus as needs became apparent. To allow for this, the architects did not produce a limiting pattern or formal plan, but rather a scheme for continuing expansion limited only to the boundaries of the site. They worried for a moment that the unity of the ultimate campus would be sacrificed for the expedient of flexibility, but with the pressures of the baby boom generation coming to university and the success of Co-operative education still unknown, the university could not afford to commit to an all-encompassing single plan.

A "Cell" or "Quadrangle" approach was at the heart of their plan for the campus. "Few finer examples of articulation of space exist than the Harvard Yards," the architects suggested, noting that the "Yards" around which Harvard University was developed were "relatively small spaces by some campus standards."[34] Applying this to Waterloo, Faculty growth would occur within cells, with each Faculty, Residence, or Church College Cell forming a campus unit of its own, designed for the buildings and the people using them. For the "colleges" built on land sloping down to the stream on the far side of Laurel Creek, Shore and Moffat suggested a pattern similar to other great university campuses noting, for example, that "[the colleges which can also be residential] are adaptable to the cellular growth pattern in a way similar to the colleges and quadrangles at Oxford and Cambridge Universities."[35] Following the examples of

Harvard, Oxford, and Cambridge, Waterloo would be one of the great university campuses.

With its open Common large enough to be a dominant space for the entire university, the knoll, or natural high point, was selected by Shore and Moffat as the campus centre. They proposed that the University Library be built there, along with an administration building and perhaps a Convocation Hall that would clearly mark this as a university space and a visual focal point. This would be the most prominent part of the campus, with each cell having direct access to the Common. The grassy knoll rising above the Chemistry and Chemical Engineering building and the location of the Physics and Mathematics building were anchor points around which proposed locations of the centre would revolve. Perhaps equally important in the 1958 plan was that, except under very restrictive circumstances, vehicular traffic would not be permitted on the campus centre or in any of the sub-units. Instead, a peripheral ring road would be the main route for traffic, with side service roads for the buildings within a cell or quadrangle. This campus would not be dominated by automobiles.[36] Traffic would occur on the edge, as Alan Adlington later expressed it, "so as to allow people to walk through the campus with their hands behind their back as university people properly should."[37] Finally, the internal aspect of the campus would be designed to offer an environment in which landscaped walks provided a pleasant and restful pedestrian circulation throughout the academic area. Academic quadrangles would be interconnected so that one might move from one to the other, passing between and around buildings and across open commons.

From the beginning, Waterloo's buildings did not provide the architectural impression that University College or Hart House did at the University of Toronto.[38] Those buildings reflected Toronto's Victorian beginnings and Vincent Massey's love of Oxford University's architecture. Waterloo was a university built in the post-war era with new ideas and new conceptions of the social role of universities in Canadian society. Waterloo was a self-consciously new university, and each spring, as the campus emerged from winter, its students would be inspired by new ideas and a sense that they, too, could make a difference. A simple philosophy for a university, but one that seemed in keeping with the spirit of Waterloo. For so many Canadians of this era who saw the Canadian landscape as an expression of Canadian identity in art and literature, the Waterloo landscape was as important as the architectural design of its buildings. Efficient, modern, using the latest building materials, they were erected at a hectic pace to meet the University's surging enrollment. Waterloo's students would not be overhelmed by the traditions of other universities.

In the Shore and Moffat philosophy, each building would "provide the best possible background for the provision of knowledge rather than [serve] as monuments in the community."[39] Within each cell or quadrangle, buildings would be alike in style and colour, and cells would differ from each other slightly to preserve a similar look to the whole campus. The requirements of speed also determined the nature of building development: buildings were needed in a hurry, and for a university without a development fund or alumni to contribute to its alma mater, buildings would be simple and practical, and built within the budget that was allowed. The first building, Chemistry and Chemical Engineering, now the Douglas Wright Engineering Building, was completed and ready for students in less than eight months – a record difficult to equal on any university campus, let alone one that was so rough and unkempt.

Like many people of his age, Hagey preferred a more traditional university building program, perhaps even one of monumental buildings with Doric or Ionian columns, oak panels and leaded windows, stone facing, and ivy on the walls. At the same time, he was driven by the need to provide classrooms and teaching buildings for those whom Waterloo sought to serve. He acquiesced in the building program without entirely endorsing it, as many others on the Board of Governors readily accepted the pragmatic building styles. Neither Kitchener nor Waterloo had a legacy of monumental buildings and the University's buildings fit within that tradition. Premier Leslie Frost often expressed his admiration for the cost-effective way that the University of Waterloo erected its buildings. He liked the Waterloo style. And in an era when Leslie Frost made the decisions about grants to universities, it was important that he support Waterloo's building program.

Mike Brooks outlined the Waterloo philosophy in January 1959. "The greatest regard," he explained, "must be paid to the spaces between buildings and the relationship of one to another." "Imaginative treatment of these spaces is essential. Landscape, the treatment of levels, of planting, of verges and terraces, roads and road furniture must all be regarded as of vital importance. ...By the careful use of landscaping and by the inter-relationship of buildings, a campus centre which will be both seen and sensed must be established...subsidiary points of emphasis must be provided. The traditional method – the use of inspiring architectural style – is now not feasible. Instead, building inter-relationships, the sensitive use of space and imaginative variety in architecture must fulfill this visual need."[40]

Landscape was the most important feature in the design of the university's campus and Shore and Moffat recommended that Hideo Sasaki, one of the most influential landscape architects in the latter half of the twentieth century, be engaged to assist them in this crucial aspect of the campus. Sasaki was a superb choice. Chairman of the Department of Landscape Architecture at Harvard University, Hideo Sasaki's philosophy was to create a sense of harmony between the campus and the larger Waterloo County environment.[41] He came to Waterloo in May, 1960 and was favourably impressed with the potential of the campus and with the concepts that Shore and Moffat had in place, modestly remarking that he almost felt as if he were talking himself out of a job.[42] Far from it, his insights provided the inspiration for developing Waterloo's landscape and ensuring that building designs were integrated into the natural setting, rather than dominating it. Like Shore and Moffat, Hideo Sasaki felt that the knoll should be retained as the campus centre and that Laurel Creek was integral to the campus landscape. He stressed that the approach to the landscape design should be naturalistic, rather than formal, fitting the topography of the area surrounding the university. Paths should be sinuous and winding rather than geometric and linear. Sculpted mounds and evergreen and deciduous planting would provide variation in the visual landscape and hide unwanted views from the campus (for example, the industrial buildings that then existed across the CNR line). To this end, trees should also obscure some views and suggest others. He emphasized that the retention of the natural state of the campus centre was important to the general landscape and that the main entrance to the university would be made to wind around the knoll rather than go over it. He also provided very specific details about the size and shape of the contours of the berms and where he wished to see them on the campus. Harold Seegmiller, whose father's company, E. and E. Seegmiller, brought in grading equipment to level the land to grade, amusingly recalled that this was the only time that his company had been "asked to put the hills back."

Ironically, as Sasaki and Brookes met with Shore and Moffat, the play of old world politics and religious disputes was being debated at an extraordinary meeting of the Evangelical Lutheran Synod in the Parish Hall of St. Peter's Lutheran Church in Kitchener. Until this moment,

the plan for the university campus included a strong Lutheran presence. The President of Waterloo College, Herbert Axford, had explored the campus site, and pointing to the area where, in later years, the Minota Hagey residence was built, Axford declared, "This is where I am going to build my Lutheran College."[43] Not only were these lands officially designated for the Lutheran college, but the central knoll, the most important location on the campus, was also reserved for the Lutheran Church. When the Evangelical Lutheran Synod voted on May 12, 1960 not to join the University of Waterloo, many in the community, and especially President Hagey, were deeply disappointed and discouraged. They had worked so hard to develop a university campus that included Waterloo College. A majority of the Waterloo College Board of Governors resigned in frustration and twenty-four of the thirty-five full time members of the faculty at Waterloo College lodged a protest against the actions of the Evangelical Lutheran Synod. Some University of Waterloo professors, however, felt a profound sense of liberation. Mathematics Professor Ralph Stanton recalls that he and Physics Professor Arthur Cowan were in Ottawa when they heard of the Synod's decision and they were "euphoric." The University of Waterloo was now free to move forward without troubled relationships of the past to hinder them.[44]

There was no longer any need to provide a link to the campus of Waterloo College. The limitations for campus planning for the University of Waterloo were removed. Hagey immediately designated the knoll as the site for the university's central building, and he declared the 10 acres of land reserved for the Lutheran College would be general university lands no longer available for any sectarian use.[45] In the meantime, the ninety-five-year-old St. Jerome's College, which had achieved independent university status in March 1959 at the same time as the Act of Incorporation created the University of Waterloo and Waterloo Lutheran University, entered into a federation agreement with the University of Waterloo as a "founding college of the new university" and made provisions to build its College and that of Notre Dame College on the university campus. St. Jerome's was soon joined by the Anglican Church-sponsored Renison College, the United Church's St. Paul's College and the Mennonite Conrad Grebel College. Located on the West side of Laurel Creek on one of the most scenic vistas of the campus, the colleges embraced Sasaki's landscape

design as their architects worked closely with Brookes to ensure building styles that were separate from, but consonant with the rest of the campus.

THE THEATRE OF THE ARTS

After the prolonged battle with his church over the campus development, President Hagey made little comment when he presented the planning documents to the Board of Governors and stated simply that he hoped the board would employ the thinking of the architects' report to make the fundamental decisions of campus planning.[46] The development of Waterloo's campus moved forward with renewed immediacy. An Arts Building, now Modern Languages, was opened in 1962 and it housed the entire Faculty of Arts, its lecture rooms, and the Theatre of the Arts. This building also illustrated the important role of the Faculty of Arts and its place on the campus. At a time when the expression of Canadian culture through art, history, music, and literature was coming to the fore, the Arts building indicated that in addition to its Science and Co-operative Applied Science programs, the University of Waterloo also valued a broadly-based humanistic tradition. The Theatre of the Arts, modeled after the then newly opened Festival Theatre in Stratford, is an important cultural link between the larger Canadian community and the University of Waterloo, and like so many events in the University's history, the origin and creation of the Theatre of the Arts has entered into the University of Waterloo's set of urban myths. Mike Brookes recalls it this way:

In late 1960 we started planning the University's first arts faculty building and it was accepted that an auditorium to hold around 500 people was badly needed and should be included in this building. Funds for building were in short supply and so it seemed sensible to try to ensure that the auditorium would serve as many purposes as possible and thereby achieve an economic level of use. In 1960 all our buildings were devoted to Science and Engineering and campus life was, for want of a better way of putting it, a bit short on humanizing influences. An auditorium, I thought, might be the opportunity not only to provide an interesting space for large gatherings but also to make some modest provisions for music, drama, debate, and gallery display and at the same time generate some activities which would attract local interest and participation.

My wife and I were well acquainted with the Stratford theatre [the Festival Theatre had in fact opened in 1957 and its revolutionary thrust stage had created a sense of excitement in the Canadian Arts community] and it seemed that a similar layout on a smaller scale might meet most of University's needs without making compromises.

As with most things then, the first step was to consult Al Adlington, our bold Vice President Finance, without whom UW would not have come about. Al always took an open-minded and constructive approach to a proposition. If it was a good idea Al supported it, even though it might be far from clear (at any rate to me) how it would be paid for.

At about that time Al, Doris Lewis and I attended a conference on library planning at Kent State University. I suppose we must have been conferring with excessive zeal because we missed our evening meal and so we walked down into Kent … when we spotted a distant illuminated sign – "Wine and Spaghetti". Ah, I remember it well. It was in this mellowing climate that, with the use of pen and paper napkin, I sought Al and Doris's views on building an apron stage theatre. They liked the idea and so with Al's blessing I set about sounding wider opinion…

On the matter of a Theatre I was confident that the Humanities folk would be supportive, but felt that Engineers might say that the cost was not justified, even if it was not hugely more than the cost of a plain auditorium. I was wrong. Engineering and Science supported the idea with enthusiasm and few qualifications, whereas Humanities showed a singular lack of interest…. A Professor of English I recall, unshakeable in his belief that a mini Globe was in mind, announced that Shakespeare was poetry, not drama, as far as he was concerned, quite possibly a popular view in some esoteric quarters, so he could not support the idea. All rather surprising.

Shore and Moffat were engaged as Architects and fascinating meetings ensued. We approached Michael Langham, then the Artistic Director of the Stratford Theatre, and he was very helpful indeed. We visited Stratford and learned a great deal about the nuts and bolts of theatre design. Michael Langham came over to Waterloo to discuss details on a model which Shore and Moffat had had constructed. We had a visit from Tanya Moseivitch (Tyrone Guthrie's designer) and spent most of a day with Robertson Davies discussing how to use the theatre to the best advantage; I don't remember much of what we concluded at that meeting but I somehow wound up buying a 5-year subscription to a rather far out magazine he edited.[47]

The matter did not end there, nor does the University's folklore. As construction progressed and the theatre began to take shape, Brookes approved of a necessary and somewhat expensive array of theatre lighting. On learning of this, somewhat after the fact, President Hagey was overheard expressing extreme displeasure. Brookes was both frustrated and angered since his relationship with Hagey had always been close and personal. McMaster University was at that very moment advertising for a property manager for its campus. Brookes called McMaster and was invited for an interview. On learning of this, Hagey was perplexed. The last thing that he wanted was to lose Brookes. Although Brookes, too, had decided that the last thing he wanted to do was to leave Waterloo, Hagey called and offered a substantial increase in salary for him to remain at Waterloo along with the promise that future campus plans would be discussed openly between the two of them. Brookes was delighted with the outcome, and building continued at its hectic pace. The Waterloo campus had its Theatre of the Arts.

From the University of Toronto's Symphony Orchestra, which performed at the opening of the Theatre of the Arts, to Waterloo's early classical orchestra directed by Maestro Alfred Kuntz, from the folk music and protest songs of " the Travelers" to early dramatic productions, the Theatre of the Arts became a center of cultural interest beyond the university community. Citizens from the surrounding areas embraced the theatre so greatly that in the early years they made up as much as half of the audience. When Canada's national touring theatre company, the Canadian Players, performed George Bernard Shaw's Arms and the Man and Shakespeare's Twelfth Night in 1963, they described the theatre "as one of the best legitimate stage theatres in Canada," in which "actors seem to have an intimate link with the audience."[48] Their performance was also the occasion for a formal dinner hosted by Kitchener business leader Henry C. Krug and his wife Mrs. Mabel Krug, which was attended by

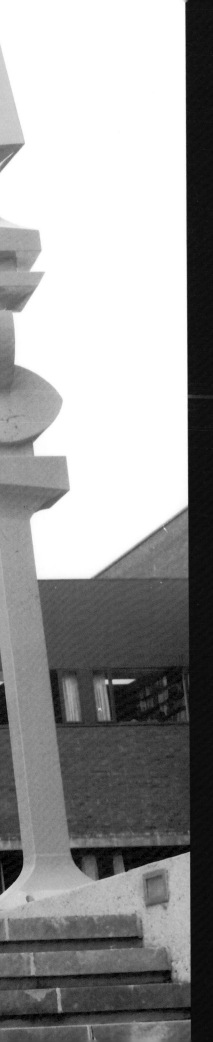

Lady Eaton, founder and honorary president of the Canadian Players Foundation and Lady Robinson, a member of the Foundation's board of directors, along with leaders from the University of Waterloo and its colleges, including both Mr. and Mrs. A. K. Adlington and Mr. and Mrs. E.M. Brookes. That the Adlingtons and the Brookes were present was particularly fitting, for without them the Theatre of the Arts might never have existed.

In the tradition of the renowned "Spring Thaw," the University of Waterloo's Faculty, Administration, Staff, and Students, led by Alan Adlington and mathematics professor Kenneth Fryer, introduced FASS night performances bringing together the university community to celebrate and to poke fun at each other. In the theatre's hushed space we have also mourned the loss of loved and distinguished colleagues, just as we have celebrated convocation and university achievements. The former Prime Minister of Canada, the Rt. Hon. John Turner has spoken here of Canada's first prime minister, the Rt. Hon. Sir John A. Macdonald; at other events, historians, political scientists, diplomats, and cabinet ministers have probed the ambiguities of Prime Minister Mackenzie King's leadership, Lester Pearson's peacemaking, and

Pierre Trudeau's spirituality. Northrop Frye discussed "the Great Code" and biblical theory; theologian Gregory Baum addressed the origins of ecumenism; Canadian astronaut and former Waterloo graduate student Chris Hatfield described the mysteries of outer space, and St. Jerome's English scholar, Eric McCormack, probed the mysteries of inner space in his novel The Mysterium. The Canadian Players have performed Shakespeare in modern garb, and the St. Aethowold's Players returned to an earlier medieval tradition. All five university presidents – Gerald Hagey, Burton Matthews, Douglas Wright, James Downey, and David Johnston – have been on its "stage" to address the university community. The Theatre of the Arts has rightly earned a place in the university's history.

AN EXPANDED CAMPUS

An exciting and innovative statement characterized the verve of the Faculty of Arts at Waterloo when in its 1962 Academic Calendar it told prospective students of an opportunity not only to share in the usual activities characterizing student and academic life of the University, but also "to be part of the development of those ideas and activities which will become in the years ahead the traditions of the University." This challenging aspect of life at the University of Waterloo "is one which gives opportunity for creative thinking for students presently enrolled and for those who enroll in the immediate years ahead." The optimism about Waterloo's role as a new Ontario university was manifest the following year when President Hagey announced that the University had purchased an additional 800 acres of land to complete the University campus, forming a continuous link from the centre of the city, through Waterloo Park, and across an expanded campus to the newly created conservation lands.

In 1965, President Hagey travelled throughout Ontario with the plans of the University of Waterloo campus in his briefcase, extolling the ideas for the university's development. On March 29, he was the keynote speaker at the Preston Chamber of Commerce's annual meeting. As was his custom, Hagey identified the number of local students who attended Waterloo, and he waxed enthusiastically about the possible future growth of the campus. It is interesting to see firsthand President Hagey's sense of the University's future growth:

"To the north of the existing South campus," he explained, "is an additional 800 acres on which it is expected there may be a North and a West campus. On the southern campus … we estimate that we can accommodate up to 8, 000 students with only two or three buildings being higher than three stories. Our present thinking is that if the

University develops beyond an enrolment of 8, 000, we would then provide for the next 8, 000 additional enrolment on either the North or West campus. Thus, if the enrolment grows to 24, 000 – and this is a possibility – the development of the total campus would be similar to that of three universities adjoining each other and being under one administration, rather than one large 24, 000-student university. Through this type of development, we will be able to offer the advantages of relatively small universities to all students on each campus and overcome many of the difficulties usually associated with a large university.[49] Even an optimist like President Hagey could not have anticipated that forty years later the University's North Campus would be the home to a major Research and Technology Park as well as a residential university village for graduate students from Canada and around the world.[50]

As the new campus lands were being added, President Hagey began to fret about the look of the existing campus. He was embarking on a scheme that was second to none in the province of Ontario, creating a university that would rival Canada's older, long established schools. So it was that he began to worry aloud about the "somewhat plain design" of the proposed Chemistry and Biology Building, and he was quite correct in his assessment. The architects had been forewarned by Brookes, who explained in the building brief, "The exterior materials and architectural style of the building will, it is felt, present the architects with their most difficult problem on this campus to date. The proximity of the Physics & Mathematics building and the possible construction of a library link might justify conformity with the architectural style of the engineering cell. It is felt, however, that this conformity would create such a dominant mass of buildings of similar character that, in the future, it would be extremely difficult for any other cell of buildings to achieve anything more than a sub-servient character. It is hoped therefore that the character of this building will harmonize with, but be different from, our existing buildings. …We wish, of course, to pursue our existing policy of providing concrete frame structures in which the quality of materials, low maintenance and functional excellence are regarded as being of foremost importance."[51]

This in turn led to a more general discussion about the campus plan. Hagey was worried that the campus would be too austere, that there was not enough variation between the buildings, and that the landscape was too undeveloped.

Hagey also wanted to be able to drive into the campus. He had always parked his car, at first a Cadillac and then in later years a Lincoln, next to his office. This was appropriate to the position of a university president: a sign that one had been successful in life. If it was done this way in business, why not at a university? When Governor General Georges Vanier visited the university, President Hagey wanted to show him the campus, but was frustrated by its inaccessibility, and he did not like that the landscaping was mostly between the buildings and not visible from the ring road. However attractive this was to students and faculty members, the beauty of the campus should be more outwardly visible. Hagey also objected that there was no identifiable entrance to the buildings from the ring road. All these years later these remain a concern for visitors to the campus. Few, however, share his worry about restricting automobiles from the centre of the campus and most agree with the importance to the overall campus design of pedestrians being able to walk throughout the campus without the infringement of traffic. Though the problems are less at Waterloo than at many other universities, automobile traffic and parking lots are part of the 21st century university landscape.

Mike Brookes attempted to assuage the president's concerns, reminding him that the landscaping which was so central to this university's character needed time to mature and that it was "well within the bounds of possibility to provide the visitor driving through the campus with, at some points, a view into a quadrangle, and at other points, the strong suggestion that by getting out of his car and walking through a colonnade or under an arch, he will see something well worth looking at. Once visitors are out of their car, they will, it is hoped, be led from one point to another by a continuance of interest. Just as visitors should see something to arouse their interest, they should not see everything at once, but should be intrigued by a continuous variation in landscape and architecture."[52] Entrances for buildings were not off of the ring road, Brookes explained, because the majority of the traffic for each building was from the campus centre, and he reminded the president that access by automobile to the centre of the campus was possible for important visitors, if not as simple and immediate as President Hagey wanted. He also assured him that the plans for the University Library (named in honour of Dana Porter, the University's first Chancellor) took into consideration the problem of architectural variation and that it would distinctly depart from, and create a contrast to, what was already on site.[53]

THE DANA PORTER LIBRARY

The Dana Porter Library is a statement that Waterloo had come of age as a university – a university that takes research seriously, where professors and graduate students toil together. The architectural brief explained: "A university library must be more than a store house, providing a passive service for members of the University community. It must inspire initial curiosity and the continuing active interest of the undergraduate student ... It should be attractive, convenient, and comfortable, inviting to its clientele, and the building should be located, oriented, and planned to this end. [Because of its relationship to the campus centre,] this building can afford to be of a distinctive architectural character. We envision the library as a major point of emphasis which will express the philosophy of function stated in this brief. ...[T]he library should present an inviting approach on all sides, but that all approaches should lead naturally to only one entrance to the building proper," avoiding the "insipid character" found at so many other

university libraries.[54] The stylized arches in the first story create the suggestion of a cloister in medieval universities, while the upper stories not only appear modern and functional, but are expressly designed to be so.

Originally, the building was to be three storeys, with additional space added as needed; almost immediately after opening in the fall of 1965, it became necessary to add the additional six storeys, symbolizing the frenetic growth of the University of Waterloo in the 1960s. As a further indication that the university had come of age, the Dana Porter Library also contributed to one of Waterloo's enduring urban myths: that the building height originally had to be halted at three storeys because the architects had not calculated the weight of the 58,000 books moved from the Physics and Mathematics building and the building was sinking.

In 1970 the Dana Porter Library rose to its planned height of nine storeys, visible from across the campus and from the historic intersection of Albert and University where the university idea had begun. The Porter Library's Special Collections department houses rare books from within Canada and around the world, and also the papers of many prominent families who assisted in establishing the university. The Schneider, Dare, Motz, Bowlby, Breithaupt, Hewetson, Clark, and Clement family papers are there along with the outstanding photographic collection of the Kitchener-Waterloo Record and the papers of a wide range of community organizations. This is no ivory tower, but a place where the community and the university meet. The creation of the Doris Lewis Rare Books Room, named after the University's first librarian, and the Peter and Betty Sims Reading Room for Contemporary Materials, named after one of the founding families

of the University, further increased its community linkage. By the University's 50th anniversary in 2007, the University of Waterloo Library system, linked electronically to the university colleges, as well as to the libraries of the University of Guelph and Wilfrid Laurier, has in excess of 7 million titles and as students from around the world arrive at the University, the Dana Porter Library is ever central to the life of the campus.

The plaza in the forecourt of the Library was the focus of national attention in November 1968 when Waterloo's radical student movement protested the horrors of the war in Vietnam by napalming a dog in front of the library. News media from across Canada descended on the campus and other students reacted in horror until the moment that the students appeared with a small hibachi barbeque and a hot dog sausage ready to be ignited with napalm. At other times students stood in front of the Library protesting the presence on campus of Co-op recruiters from Dow Chemicals, while counter-demonstrators lined up on the other side of the plaza protesting the protest.

Developing Waterloo's campus required more than a collection of buildings. In an interview after he returned to England, Mike Brookes candidly remarked that "[at Waterloo] I took every brick personally."[55] And so he did. His imprint is writ large. A photograph of Stourhead Lake in England, which occupied a place of prominence in Brookes's office, became the inspiration for one of the campus's beauty spots, the small lake near Conrad Grebel University College. It was also Brookes who set out the philosophy that guided the creation of a "Student Village," the first university residence. Now Ron Eydt Village, named after the long-time "Warden" of the village, it was based on the concept of a medieval village. This was a revolutionary idea in university development, yet it was consistent with a university that saw students as integral to its future. And it was Brookes who introduced the Peacock Club to the university when he acquired four peacocks to serve as ornaments on the campus. When the university chose not to support this idea, Brookes paid for the peacocks out of his own pocket and formed the Peacock Club so that faculty and staff members might contribute to their upkeep. Brookes's intense personal involvement with the growth of the campus is not likely to be repeated.

THE RED ROOM

In 1966, the construction of the Mathematics and Computer Building introduced a new architectural firm, Webb, Zerafa, Menkes and Matthews to the Waterloo campus, and the size and scale of this building fundamentally altered the "look" and "feel" of the campus. The use of concrete rather than brick facing marked a departure from past practice and the building's style, common to universities in the late 1960s and referred to as "the new brutism," indicated a dramatic change. Six storeys high, the Mathematics and Computer Building was the largest building on the campus, meant to be a strong architectural presence, and although not a monument to an individual, it was a recognition of the importance for the University of the creation of its unique Faculty of Mathematics and Waterloo's international presence in the then newly-developing field of Computer Science. Described as "the second pivotal building on campus after the library," it was a "university" building, showcasing the IBM computer in the famous Red Room and providing computing facilities for students across the campus, in addition to housing the Engineering, Mathematics, and Science library.

In 1967, the Computing Centre moved its formidable array of equipment into the new building. The department had four computers to relocate, some quite massive: the IBM 1620, 1710 and 360/75. From the moment of its opening, the Red Room, located in the centre of the new Mathematics and Computer Building, became an icon and an attraction that brought thousands of visitors and students to the University of Waterloo. The choice of the red colour and the two storey gallery overlooking the mainframe computer is also part of Waterloo folklore and the stuff of legend. Peter Sprung, who worked in the Computing Centre, vividly recalls the reaction of the Director of the Computing Centre, Wes Graham when as he first learned of the red tiles:[56]

The architects had hired an interior decorator, but Graham, who was Director of the Computing Centre, was blissfully unaware of the implications until one day when he and I were walking over from the Physics building, we saw the red wall tiles. "Wes almost had a stroke,"

Sprung recalled. "This is awful," Wes said. "We've got to put a stop to it! Stop everything." The decorator tried to explain that "the building was a really strong architectural statement – it's masculine and has dominant outside pillars and it's grey. And the interior walls are all a neutral colour – and to add colour, she had determined that the doors would be alternately red or a very, very dark brown, which to the eye looked black... As you looked down a corridor the floor was terrazzo, the walls neutral, and splashes of colour came from the doors. And then she said, 'and the jewel – the pearl in the center of the oyster to pull all this colour together – is the red room.'" Wes was horrified. He tried to reason with her. "Well, that's an interesting idea, but you realize that the computer is blue." She said, "No it can't be blue!" ... "Well, then," she said, "we'll paint it." ..."No you can't," Wes replied, " – you can't just paint the panels on a computer. It's all special baking paint process, it just can't be done...but IBM does make a red computer." Her eyes brightened and she said, "Great, let's have a look at that." So we all traipsed down to Toronto where a red computer was installed, and she took one look at it and said, "No, no, it's the wrong red!" At this point we said, "Well, this is it, the computer's going to be blue." So we came to have a blue computer installed in a red room. And, of course, everybody could see it because the second floor was all surrounded by windows. The windows were there because, in those days, students submitted their jobs to the computer after going to a key punch room where there were 60 key punches – and students would punch their deck of cards. The top card, of course, had their identification on it. And then they would put an elastic band around those cards and leave them in a bin on the second floor where people – who were called rippers and wrappers – took the bins full of these card decks down to the computer room where they would feed the cards through the card reader, and the computer would process them and chug out the output on an online printer that printed reasonably fast. And then the rippers and wrappers would match up the paper coming off the printer with the cards that had been fed through the computer and put an elastic band around them and put them back up in an output room. ... The second floor windows were so that rather than leave their cards in a room

and get paper back later without having any idea of what was happening, the students could look down and see the cards being read in and see the paper coming off the printer and see the tape drives going around and the lights going back and forth. This was to give them an idea that this wasn't magic, that there was something actually happening down there.[57]

The array of new buildings did not end here. The Physical Activities Complex was added in 1968 along with the Campus Centre. These were both Shore and Moffat buildings and fit within the older tradition. The Campus Centre was described as "the living room of the campus" and its lofty great hall provided a much needed venue for student life on what was still a rather stark campus. A generation later, in response to demands for greater student services, a major expansion to the original building was completed by the architectural firm of Carruthers and Shaw. The Campus Centre of storied fame, a gathering place for radical students in the 1970s, became the Student Life Centre in the 1990s, another time and another place. During 1968, the year that had seen student unrest reach unprecedented levels around the world, two other important university buildings were added: the Health Services building and the Minota Hagey Residence, named in honour of President Hagey's wife, Minota, who died in 1965. These buildings were designed by Raymond Moriyama, one of Canada's most highly honoured architects and Chancellor of Brock University. After a hiatus on university construction instituted by the Ontario Government, an exception was made in 1987, when, under the presidency of Waterloo's third president, Douglas Wright, the William G. Davis Centre for Computer Research, with its stunningly different architectural style, was opened.

Designed by the IKOY partnership of Winnipeg with the Toronto firm of Mathers and Haldenby, this building was an even greater break from the original Waterloo architectural style. Built of steel and glass, its design and its presence were controversial, and at 309,000 square feet it was even larger than the original Mathematics and Computer Building. The Davis Centre nonetheless retained the quadrangle concept so critical to the Shore and Moffat campus design and in an era of doubt in universities and their societal role, the Davis Centre exhibited a sense of confidence in the future and of the commitment of the University of Waterloo to moving that future forward.

The Faculty of Applied Health Science Complex, begun originally in 1971 as B.C. Matthews Hall, with the 2005 addition designed by Stephen Teeple, combined both the quadrangle or cell concept with a sensitive integration into the landscape. The Lyle S. Hallman addition completed in 2005 spoke not only of this innovative faculty's excellence in research in the field of applied health science, but also provided a visual link between the new Research and Technology Park on the North Campus and a gateway to the architectural styles of the buildings on the South Campus. The addition to the Student Life Centre to the south reinforces the earlier architecture design, and its walkway forms a natural meeting place for student life activities, retaining the original sense of the campus. The proposed interdisciplinary Institute for Quantum Computing, now known as the Quantum Nano Centre, on the green between the Mathematics and Computer Building, the Sciences Complex, and the Student Life Centre, will complete the cell or quadrangle campus design set out nearly fifty years earlier.

In an earlier era, embroiled in the everyday reality of creating a university, President Hagey remarked that at Waterloo they were setting a course that looked to the future, rather than one that was based on past university precedents. "Major changes in established universities are difficult," he had said. "Many of the major changes that have been made in higher education programs during the last century have developed through new colleges rather than through previously established universities. Consequently, Waterloo, in organizing a new university, is challenged to develop courses in line with our country's present and future needs. Waterloo has an opportunity to do something about the present and future needs quickly; through established universities, radical changes would be materially more difficult."[58]

Looking back at the hurried pace of events during the first year of the Associate Faculties, Hagey recalled this was probably "the shortest time in which a major education project such as this has been organized; except in times of war emergencies. During this past year, this institution has received more national publicity than many of our large universities. The development of our co-operative courses is probably being followed with more interest than any other course in Canada... [and] As a relatively small institution, we have undertaken a program... the magnitude of which, in relation to our size, is probably without precedent. One might say that we have staked our claim in an area with a large known potential. Now our job is to develop that claim, and most of our energies should be directed toward that objective during the coming year."[59] In March 1957, Hagey reported to the Board of Governors about what had been one of the most remarkable twelve months of his life. "This past year, nearly everything has had to be done under more pressure than is desirable," he began. "This has necessitated bypassing many channels that should normally be followed." "Frankly," he admitted, "the job has been running your administrators, rather than vice versa. We are certainly conscious of the need to correct this situation as quickly as possible."[60] The pace of development over the next years only increased.[61]

Mike Brookes recalls standing with President Hagey on the front steps of the Schweitzer Farm-house where the two of them met regularly, often over coffee, watching the developing campus. Hagey turned to him, and said that if he had known what the university would become, he doubted that he would have had the courage to begin.[62] Few others had Hagey's pluck and determination to make education available to Ontario's students, but even he was daunted by the adventure in which he was engaged. But Hagey, once described as "someone who dreamed in Technicolor," had carried on his dream and purchased the 733 acre North Campus.

RESEARCH AND TECHNOLOGY

Under the leadership of the University's fifth president, David Johnston, a product of education at the Harvard Yard and the Quadrangles of Cambridge University in England, Waterloo has pushed forward into the next century, still surrounded by the fields of Mennonite farm lands settled some two hundred years ago. In silent testimony stands the John E. Brubacher 1856 Farmhouse, where the Mennonite pioneering spirit commingles with a strikingly different pioneering spirit of the 21st century. This, too, is the University of Waterloo. The juxtaposition of Mennonite farms and a university in the vanguard of technological advances is now commonplace as Waterloo has gone from a vague idea, shoehorned onto a campus of less than 30 acres, to the largest integrated university campus in Ontario. The University's Research and Technology Park, anchored by two University of Waterloo spin-off companies, Sybase and Open Text, and accompanied by a new Accelerator Centre to encourage the development of university-related ideas in the marketplace, have begun the commercial development of another area of the North Campus. For all of that, fifty years after the first building was hurriedly constructed the original

Engineering Quad is still visible as the Faculty of Engineering has grown from the Chemistry and Chemical Engineering building (later known as Engineering I and later still as the Douglas Wright Engineering Building), to Engineering II and Engineering III added in 1961, the J.R. Coutts Engineering Lecture Hall in 1967, the Carl A. Pollock Hall in 1971, and the Centre for Environmental and Information Technology in 2003. The latter building is a natural "crossroads" between the Biology and Chemistry complex, the original Shore and Moffat Physics and Mathematics building, the Engineering Quad, and the Davis Centre for Computer Research. The spectacular Atrium, home to the Natural Sciences Museum, challenges the curiosity of its visitors as it also integrates the range of ideas in the surrounding buildings. The play of natural light through the Atrium's skylights constantly changes the character of the space. In a very real way the Centre for Environmental and Information Technology is a metaphor of the growth of the University, retaining the central character of the university with interdisciplinary links to Mathematics and Science in adjoining "cells."

THE CAMPUS – 2007

From the Science Complex, one can see the Dana Porter Library at the centre of the original knoll, with Needles Hall to the right and the Arts Quadrangle flowing past the Arts Lecture Hall to the stepped entrance to Hagey Hall of the Humanities and off to the right is the Environmental Studies building with the Robert Starbird Dorney Ecology Garden inviting passers by to stop for a moment and consider the natural beauty of its setting. From the Dana Porter plaza, one can still see the Schweitzer Farm-house, now home to the Graduate Students, reminding us of the importance of Student Life on the campus. Once standing aloof and forlorn on an abandoned farm, the Schweitzer Farm-house now echoes with student debate and discussion. To the south east is the South Campus Hall and the Tatham

Centre for Co-operative Education and Career Services. As one walks across the Science Quad toward the Student Life Centre and the Physical Education Complex another nucleus of student activity can be found. Growing and adapting as students' needs have changed over nearly half a century, the original campus plan has been remarkably resilient. Laurel Creek remains a natural spine through the campus with vistas and still-open space on the North Campus and in the South Campus it winds its way past the residences of the Ron Eydt Village and the colleges, creating a unique sense of space adapted to the natural contours of the land. The playing fields on the North Campus, the Village Green, and the Finn Green at St. Jerome's provide a venue for intramural sports. Each spring as the blossoms renew the campus, and in the autumn as the foliage brings forth its spectacular colours, the campus attracts visitors and graduates alike to the University, capturing another glimpse of the life of the university campus. Fifty years on, the campus thrives, changing with the seasons. Its attractiveness endures.

Like the campus, the University itself continues to evolve. The sense of adventure of the original "fearsome five" as they set out beyond the confines of Waterloo College was recalled when the University Senate and the Board of Governors agreed to relocate the School of Architecture to historic Cambridge – this Cambridge in Ontario, not Great Britain – on the banks of the Grand River, confirming the spirit of Waterloo. This was followed by the decision to locate a Health Sciences complex with a School of Pharmacy, a centre for Family Medicine, an Optometry Clinic, and a regional centre of McMaster's Michael De Groote School of Medicine in Kitchener. Those who think about the University's history will quickly realize that this is the site where Ira Needles once presided over B.F. Goodrich and where Gerry Hagey spent the formative years of his career before becoming President of Waterloo College. History at Waterloo has a way of linking the past with the present and setting a new course for the future. And as you will see, that, too, is part of the Waterloo story.

CHAPTER TWO

More unconventional beginnings

Vincent Bladen, Dean of Arts and Science at the University of Toronto, liked to tell his students that the University of Toronto was one of the two great universities in the English-speaking world. The other was Oxford. It is not surprising that the 32-year-old Keith Thomas, who arrived at Waterloo in May 1960, newly appointed as Acting Dean of Arts, a graduate of the University of Toronto and a former chair of the English Department at Acadia University, shared Vincent Bladen's view of Toronto's stature and that he tried to create a similar program at Waterloo. When Thomas travelled to Waterloo College the previous summer with fellow Toronto graduate Paul Cornell, also a colleague at Acadia, to inquire about job prospects, he was treated courteously by President Hagey but was told that there was little likelihood of a Faculty of Arts being established. Thomas and Cornell left their résumés with President Hagey and returned, disappointed, to Nova Scotia. In less than a year, they were hurriedly invited back to Waterloo, the former to become Chair of English and Acting Dean of Arts and Cornell to become Chair of History and Acting Chair of Economics, Political Science, and Geography.

The University of Toronto curriculum with its Anglophile predilections so admired by Thomas, however, would not take root in the University of Waterloo, which considered extending the frontiers of knowledge of greater importance than adopting the existing traditions of another university, let alone ones that harkened to Canada's colonial past. For one thing, the launch of the Soviet satellite Sputnik 1 on October 5, 1957, had challenged university traditions across the Western world, as many believed the old ways and the old universities had let us down. Vital upstart universities like the University of Waterloo were given a unique chance to prove themselves. It was not just the Soviet Union's technological success that worried western leaders; they were equally concerned about falling victim to its "ecumenical ambitions" that threatened the democratic ideals of nations like Canada.

A University Arts Faculty was seen as essential to the success of the University of Waterloo and the creation of the separate identity of its Faculty of Arts as much as the implementation of the controversial program of Co-operative education dominated discussion in the University's founding years. The idea of a university in Waterloo had come about when the Lutheran-based Waterloo College required financial support to supplement its Arts program. To access this provincial funding they intended to add science courses through the creation of a non-sectarian institution known as the "Waterloo College Associate Faculties," which was organized in 1956 under the provisions of the Ontario Small Companies Act. The Associate Faculties was "sponsored" by Waterloo College and its students could take courses through Waterloo College and share its campus facilities, but it was separately chartered with its own Board of Governors. The President of Waterloo College, Gerald Hagey, however, was also President of the Waterloo College Associate Faculties. As a non-sectarian institution, the Waterloo College Associate Faculties was eligible for Provincial Government grants for its students and capital grants to assist in erecting its buildings. It was expected that the Associate Faculties' Science buildings would be located adjacent to the Waterloo College campus, making them available to the Arts students and that Waterloo College professors would provide the Arts and Science courses for students enrolled through the Associate Faculties, thereby adding to the income stream of an already heavily burdened college and providing an Arts Faculty that would meet the Associate Faculties' needs.

It had all seemed simple enough and not terribly different from the creation of the Baptist Church-sponsored McMaster University in nearby Hamilton. Following a path similar to that of McMaster and the recently incorporated Assumption University in Windsor, a private member's bill established the University of Waterloo and created two Arts universities that were expected to "federate" or join as integral parts of the University of Waterloo. Along with Waterloo College, St. Jerome's College, a Roman Catholic college established in 1865, was to federate with the University of Waterloo. Arts students attending either Waterloo College or St. Jerome's College could take courses at the University of Waterloo, as well as within either of the other two colleges, and receive a degree from the University of Waterloo.[1]

A critical step in the creation of a separate University Faculty of Arts occurred in April 1959 when the Lutheran-based Waterloo College determined that its president, Gerald Hagey, would have to resign if he were to be President of the University of Waterloo. The integrated relationship envisioned in 1956 and the idea of Waterloo College as the Arts centrepiece of the University of Waterloo faded. The separation of the two institutions seemed even clearer with the appointment of Herbert Axford as President of Waterloo College who arrived in Waterloo in 1959, "dubious" about federation with the University of Waterloo.[2]

Some others shared Axford's doubts, but for very different reasons. One of those who did so was Ralph Stanton, chairman of the Department of Mathematics, who had come to Waterloo College from the University of Toronto in 1957 with the expectation of being part of a new university beyond the Lutheran College that employed him. Stanton urged President Hagey to establish the University of Waterloo's own unique and rigorous Arts Faculty. Frustrated with the limited Lutheran-based Arts Faculty then in existence at Waterloo College, he outlined to President Hagey a detailed plan for a "University Faculty of Arts," arguing that "in view of the increasingly unsatisfactory service provided [by Waterloo College] in the Arts Electives, it would be prudent to prepare a rough estimate of the requirements for an Arts Program."[3] He explained: "The need for a University Arts Faculty is so great, and our uniqueness among Canadian Universities in possessing no non-denomination Arts Faculty is so striking, that I am sure that all of us in the Chemistry, Physics, and Engineering Buildings [newly opened on the campus of the University of Waterloo] would be willing to squeeze up temporarily so as to provide both teaching space and office quarters for University people in the Humanities and Social Sciences … Provided we can have our Arts Faculty ready by December [1959]."[4]

Stanton believed that "there should be no difficulty in obtaining a minimum of 80 students for First Year Arts," and he added, "This would in no way injure Waterloo College, since we would expect to draw students who prefer a non-denominational institution, and who are desirous of the high standards which we would demand …"[5] This latter statement reflects Stanton's growing agitation about the failure rate in mathematics amongst Waterloo College Students and his belief that the college admitted students who were unqualified for university level work. President Hagey hesitated to take Stanton's advice, insisting that, "It was the hope of the Board [of Governors] that the University would not be forced to create a Faculty of Arts solely because of a failure to federate on the part of Waterloo College." For Stanton,

however, that was not really the point at issue. "No one," he said, "was opposed to federation with Waterloo College, merely to the dominant position of one religious college as the Faculty of Arts for the whole university." He tried to explain to President Hagey that, "…whereas all persons are desirous of seeing a proper federation built up, it would be a valuable complement to federation if the University were to create its own Faculty of Arts at the same time. [This] would put us on the Toronto model, and would have great virtue for our future development … Such a move would actually tend to allay certain fears on the part of the Lutheran Church if it were suitably presented, since if there were a University Faculty of Arts, which was non-denominational, then there would be no need nor danger of any persons pressing for the secularization of the Lutheran-related College."[6] The latter issue had come to worry some of the leaders of the "Lutheran camp" about their place in the university. University politics are often volatile, but the mixture in Waterloo that year was especially combustible.

The problems surrounding Waterloo College's role as a possible Faculty of Arts for a non-sectarian institution were complicated by the actions of its dean and president. On January 25, James Sandison, a member of the English Department of Waterloo College, complained to the president of his Faculty Association that at a meeting with the College Dean, Reverend Lloyd Schaus, he was "given a very strong impression that he was dismissed" and that "the reason given for his dismissal was that his beliefs as expressed in class were not consonant with the aims (presumably religious aims) of this institution."[7] The Sandison case made many faculty members anxious and uncomfortable. The college did not have a policy on academic freedom and tenure, although faculty members had been asking for one for months. When Professor Sandison met with President Axford on February 11, concerns about religious freedom were highlighted. Axford "raised the point that the constitution of the college required that all faculty members must be 'communicant Christians'." He asked Sandison directly if he was "a communicant of any church" and whether he knew "that the constitution of Waterloo College has a clause requiring all faculty members to be Protestant communicants." When Sandison replied that he had not known this, Axford suggested that his "ignorance of the aforementioned clause in the Constitution

would work in [his] favour, though he pointed out that only yesterday a Jew had been refused a position on our faculty because of this clause."[8]

Tension rose again in April when a candidate for the German and Russian department was rejected because he was a Roman Catholic. The head of the department, J.W Dyck, resigned in protest and, he and his newly rejected colleague, Edmund Heier, were immediately appointed to the University of Waterloo.[9] A statement of Waterloo College's policy on academic freedom and tenure was made public on May 9, confirming the Lutheran orientation of the College. Over the signature of President Axford, the document explained: "Teachers are reminded that the College is an agency of the Lutheran Church, and is to be used as an opportunity for teachers to bring the light of the divinely inspired truth of the Holy Scriptures into the compass of their students."[10] The administration had taken a strongly pro-Lutheran position in the face of federation with a non-denominational university. This made many in the former Associate Faculties decidedly uncomfortable and it strengthened their resolve to push for a separate University of Waterloo Arts Faculty. Then, in a moment of great drama, at the Extraordinary Special Meeting of the Evangelical Lutheran Synod in Kitchener on May 12, despite President Hagey's assurances of the importance of their college in the new University of Waterloo, the Lutheran Synod overturned the January decision of its own Board of Governors and rejected the federation agreement with the University of Waterloo.[11] Many non-Lutheran faculty members sought to join the University of Waterloo. Others, like historian Geoff Adams, simply left hoping for academic postings at other Canadian or American universities. Still others, like English Professor Flora Roy, remained at Waterloo College. It would take years for suspicion and rancour to diminish between the two institutions. One thing was clear, the University of Waterloo would have to establish its own Arts Faculty and it would have to do so immediately.

With less than one month before the University's first convocation – some had doubted that an Arts Faculty could be put in place so quickly – the appointment of Keith Thomas as Acting Dean of Arts and the creation of an Arts Faculty was announced in newspapers across Ontario. On Saturday, June 18, 1960, barely one month after the forced separation with Waterloo College, the Honourable Dana Porter, Q.C., B.A., M.A., Chief Justice of Ontario, who as the former Treasurer of Ontario had overseen the dramatic beginnings of this new institution, was installed as the first Chancellor of the University of Waterloo. The *Kitchener-Waterloo Record* captured the excitement, describing the installation, held on a temporary dais in the Seagram Gymnasium, as "a colourful ceremony dating back to Middle Ages Scholasticism."[12] In his inaugural address, replete with references to the learning of past ages, Chancellor Porter happily noted that "in addition to the provision made for the Sciences, the University has now established an Arts Faculty which will open this autumn." "This is indeed a great achievement in so short a time," said the chancellor, as he set out to bestow an honorary degree upon University of Western Ontario history professor and chief librarian James. J. Talman. Dana Porter's commitment to the excitement and innovation of University of Waterloo was enduring. His relationship with the school was made clear when he was later asked to allow his name to stand as a candidate for Chancellor of his alma mater, the University of Toronto. He demurred, and ultimately declined, explaining that his "loyalty" to Waterloo took precedence.[13]

ACTING DEAN KEITH THOMAS AND THE ARTS CURRICULUM

Although Keith Thomas's appointment as Acting Dean of Arts was confirmed on May 20, 1960, Thomas had not sought the deanship. In February 1960 he wrote to the Registrar of the University of Waterloo, A.P. Gordon, merely asking about the possibility of the chairmanship of a future English department since F.E.L. Priestly, his mentor at the University of Toronto and an acquaintance of Ralph Stanton's, had suggested that Waterloo was now considering plans for establishing a Faculty of Arts. "This has whetted my curiosity no end," Thomas explained to Gordon, and "I should greatly appreciate it if you would let me know whether your plans have changed [since the previous summer] or whether you would entertain such an application."[14] Gordon forwarded the letter to Bruce Kelley, who, in the midst of the then on-and-off-again federation negotiations with Waterloo Lutheran

University, had been appointed by the University of Waterloo as Dean of Science and Acting Dean of Arts. Kelley kept in touch with Thomas, telling him in April that "We who are now at the University of Waterloo are here in the capacity of pioneers, and as such are willing to put up with unfortunate discomforts that are the lot of the pioneer. I am afraid that for the next year or two pioneering will continue to be the order of the day."[15] No offer was made, since the protracted federation negotiations with Waterloo College were still ongoing. Then on May 9, in a meeting with President Hagey, Bruce Kelley died of a massive heart attack. The University lost a senior scholar and mediator. There was no one from Waterloo who could step in and take his place, until, on May 20, President Hagey announced that Dr. Keith Thomas from Acadia University would be Chairman of English and Acting Dean of the Faculty of Arts at the University of Waterloo.[16]

Thomas later suggested that he was given the position as Acting Dean perhaps because he was the only applicant with administrative experience. He described the University of Waterloo as a having a "most exhilarating atmosphere…; a great opportunity to build a new university and what [he] had in mind was to attempt to create, in arts, a system that would be even more demanding than at U of T."[17] Keith Thomas had very definite ideas about what he wanted in a Faculty of Arts. He was especially keen to apply this idea to general arts, as he believed honours students throughout Canada looked down upon general arts and he felt that, with a carefully devised curriculum, it could be virtually as demanding as an honours program.[18] An informal committee, which included representatives from St. Jerome's, previously meeting sub rosa at Dean Bruce Kelley's home, had prepared a Waterloo Arts Faculty program including a mimeographed calendar. Once Thomas arrived, he set about creating an entirely new curriculum and by July, he had drafted a daunting thirteen-page memo to all members of the Faculty of Arts, outlining the principles on which he would base his curriculum: the provision of breadth of study, the representative sampling of various disciplines, the coming into contact with both the historical context of our civilisation's ideas and at least one analysis of present society, an introduction to the principles and methods of the various sciences, a deeply penetrating study within a major discipline, and the integration of various subjects and courses into one unified whole.[19]

Thomas was an unabashed elitist in his approach to Arts education. Desiring a visual connection to an ancient arts tradition, he chose to wear a lecturer's gown when he began teaching at the University.[20] Not all of the faculty members in this new university welcomed Thomas's approach. In August, a hastily-assembled Arts Faculty Council meeting debated his suggested curriculum, proposing instead that each department prepare programs that they deemed suitable for their students and then present them to him.[21] Stanton spoke out most strongly on the impacts of Thomas's curriculum on Mathematics students, especially opposing the formal compulsory requirement of a "classical subject" for all Arts students.[22] Like Thomas, Stanton had graduated from and taught at the University of Toronto, and while he respected the Toronto tradition in Arts and Science, he felt that Toronto had become set in its ways, that opportunities for advancement were limited, and that in numerical analysis and finite mathematics as well as in computing applications, Toronto was stagnating. He also knew that some of the brightest and best graduate students from the University of Toronto could easily be recruited to come to Waterloo, but not if Waterloo was only to follow where Toronto had led and that Waterloo would succeed as a university only if it moved out of the shadow of Toronto's orthodoxy.

Soon after Thomas's arrival, President Hagey recognized problems were likely to ensue. He attempted to halt the debate on Thomas's proposed curriculum by suggesting a delay in implementation until December, to allow for a careful exploration of all ideas.[23] Discussion continued throughout the fall with little support for Thomas's plan. In February 1961, a frustrated Keith Thomas withdrew his name from consideration for the permanent position as Dean of the Faculty of Arts. Reflecting on this period of his career, Thomas suggested that the composition of the Arts Faculty made it very difficult to accomplish his goal. The "artsmen" could not come to an agreement among themselves with respect to curriculum, while the members of the Department of Mathematics, who outnumbered all others, took their lead from Stanton, who "had his own ideas."[24] Keith Thomas's term as Acting Dean, however short, had inadvertently influenced the direction of the Arts faculty so that it became highly individualized, with new ways of presenting Arts subjects taking precedence over older methods taught at other universities. Never was it to be the integrated, elitist program modelled on the University of Toronto that Thomas had envisioned.

Thomas argued in his letter of resignation that "there would be no continuing creativity in the position of Deanship: all the creative work that remains to be done will be done in the departments and by individuals."[25] There was much that was true in this statement. Inevitably, the strength of the Arts Faculty depended on the strength of its individual department chairs, much like the strength of the University in the beginning depended on its deans. The die was cast. Waterloo was set to move in its own direction, and it was one that Hagey saw as successful in mathematics and engineering – why not in Arts, too?

With Thomas's curriculum defeated, and his resignation in 1961, the university began to search for a new Dean of Arts. Of the faculty's suggestions, Stanton's nominees were the most numerous. He proposed seeking a social scientist as the next Dean, someone who "would contribute a breadth of knowledge which pure humanists in fields such as English and Philosophy frequently lack."[26] Agreeing with the Dean of Engineering, Douglas Wright, Stanton felt that the "avoidance of a narrow outlook is very important."[27] The narrow outlook that Stanton wanted to avoid was one that would establish requirements for students across the entire faculty, as Thomas had proposed. Why then should the Dean not be Ralph Stanton who had a second PhD in Portuguese and who was in contact with scholars in language and literature throughout the United States and Great Britain? Stanton, it seems, was more interested in preserving his position as Chairman or Dean of Graduate Studies, in moulding the bigger picture of the university, than in becoming the Dean of Arts.[28] Besides, no one doubted that in the back rooms of the university Ralph Stanton would continue to exercise a significant influence on the direction of the Arts Faculty. No one could have anticipated just how true this was or how extensive was his influence.

NORMAN HIGH AS DEAN OF ARTS

In June 1961, President Hagey tentatively appointed Norman High as the Dean of Arts. High had previously taught at the Agricultural school in Guelph, where he was Director of the Agricultural College's Extension Program, but he was attracted to Waterloo, especially as a leader of the Mennonite community, which was hoping to establish an affiliated College (Conrad Grebel College). W.H. Bexton, Chairman of the Psychology Department, recommended High for the position of dean.[29] Bexton suggested High because he believed that he could mend the divisions developing in the faculty and he had been "increasingly impressed by both his [High's] fair-mindedness and his ability to come directly to the core of a problem and to deal with it succinctly."[30] Father Siegfried of St. Jerome's agreed with Bexton and felt that after Thomas, High would be a good peacemaker for the faculty. High had also gained the support of a number of the other faculty members, including J.W. Dyck whose graduate program in German Thomas had opposed.[31] Dyck had recently spent an evening with High in which university politics had been vigorously discussed. "Your patient understanding for our past 'dirty laundry,'" Dyck wrote, "…convinced even our fair companion that fairer days can be expected in the future… I also had a conversation with Dr. Hagey. I think that he wants you too. Naturally, some manoeuvring is always in the air."[32] "Hagey felt that things had become so prickly under Thomas that you needed someone who was almost a pastor, to smooth things down," Stanton recalled. "Norman [High] did manage to successfully quiet down the arts faculty after a period of great turmoil."[33] Increasingly, under High, the Faculty of Arts developed a social science focus, while at the same time, High allowed the Faculty to fragment into a loose collection of independent departments. In the future, this characteristic of Arts would be problematic, but it also provided the freedom to develop several unique interdisciplinary programs.

In the summer of 1962, this independent direction for the new Arts Faculty was given a major shock when Ralph Stanton, on the advice of colleagues in Mathematics and Psychology, successfully persuaded one of the University of Toronto's most distinguished psychologists, Richard Walters, to leave Toronto and to bring with him to Waterloo several faculty members as well as their Master's students. With the tacit agreement of Dean High, Stanton not only recruited Walters to be the Chairman of the department of Psychology, but he also left the department chairman, W.H. Bexton, completely in the dark. Stanton reasoned that with Walters in the faculty, the prestige of the University would dramatically increase, and besides, Bexton's term was up for renewal "prior to August 1963."[34] Overnight, Waterloo's department acquired an international reputation. [35]Not surprisingly, Bexton lamented Stanton's coup, complaining: "Professional ethics, and common courtesy, would indicate that a full professor and the senior member of a department should be consulted before an approach is made to any individual being considered as an addition to a department. Such consultations would seem to be all the more pertinent when the senior person involved has served the institution since its inception and has been responsible for the development of the policy and program in the department."[36] Bexton resigned twelve days into 1963.[37]

Appointed as the first Chairman of Graduate Studies, and later as Dean of Graduate Studies, Ralph Stanton persuaded President Hagey that if Waterloo was to be accepted as a university of the first rank, graduate research and teaching must be a sine qua non of the Waterloo experience. Scepticism of other universities about the academic reputation of Co-operative education meant that, from the beginning, Waterloo felt it necessary to be a research-intensive university with strong graduate programs. This was an essential part of its ethos. For his part, Hagey successfully fought attempts by the province to limit graduate program expansion only to the older universities such as Toronto, Queen's, and Western. President Hagey's support for rapid expansion into graduate work ensured that Arts was never seen as

merely providing service teaching for the Faculty of Engineering, and before long the enrolment in Arts would equal that of Engineering.

Faculty members were attracted to Waterloo's Arts programs by the prospect of building a new faculty where their ideas could blossom. Paul Cornell, who joined the University of Waterloo that fateful summer of 1960, successfully recruited senior colleagues to join him in the Faculty of Arts. One of those was K.A. MacKirdy, a history professor at the University of Washington in Seattle, who was interested in returning to Canada. Cornell's letter to him in February 1961 is an insightful description of the Faculty of Arts at Waterloo:

I came here,[he told MacKirdy] because on examination the promise of building a real, proper Humanities School looked good, and the sound of the people on the ground rang true. I still think the same way. The battles that we have fought have been between Arts men, this year, mainly on the lines of drawing up a curriculum. In the working out of our needs for office and teaching space we arrived at 634 as the minimum Arts enrolment in 1965. We're building, as the preliminary thinking goes at the moment, for approx 1,000 in Arts.

I don't sense the feeling that this is to be a pale copy of M.I.T., although there will have to be constant vigilance. In the budget, there is a tendency to need a computer, but to haggle about the salaries of say (yourself) a key Arts appointment. But this is a natural enough problem. There are 59 Arts students at the moment, while the university registration is 1000+. There is the inevitable banter about "unpractical" arts men, etc. But the whole faculty is young. Very few people are 40, and all the key administrators are 40ish or younger. They are quite open to experiment and co-operation on pilot schedules to bridge Arts-Sci-Eng gulfs.

The Board of Governors dream of a "proper" university... There was a great scurrying around in late spring and into the summer gathering a cadre to teach a 1st year of arts and "get off the ground." From here we must try to build in the face of a seller's market. We will be as good as the faculty we can assemble.... As to the "new league" idea - and fitting. This is one of the few cases where we can still make many of our own rules and establish our own traditions. It seems to be in the cards that humanist fields will be favoured 1st. Some of the flavour of Western Ontario, and Waterloo College lingers, for many of the people have local connections.

But the dilution will be progressive. I'll want the best advice of yourself ... to hew an optimum path in finding new faculty, and helping to give a new flavour to the new creation.

We are embarking right away, on a selective group of Honour Courses. Our curriculum is agreed to by the Dept of Education, we are able to carve out areas where we feel we should carve, without the restraining hand of a parent University. (This is rather a soul searching business; Mathematics can, and is offering graduate work, but History will have to wait till our resources are riper- but when we think we can do grad work, we can go ahead, the administrative machinery is taking shape already...).

If our 58 freshmen are a true sample, then our students will be quite challenging. I've had more lift this year, than any year at Acadia generated by student enthusiasm....

I'll send the mimeographed sheets of what is to be our 1st Arts calendar. We finally agreed to these items in a meeting last night. It is the product of many hours and committee work. It contains compromises, but these are compromises between opposing ideas within our faculty. The debate continues - everyone is involved in the debate. As we settle down, it appears that very great initiative is left to the Departments in detailing the curriculum of their own "Majors" and "Honours" students. (I would guess that we would have about 6 or 7 honour students next year (i.e. 2nd year).

In general, there is a spirit of a going concern, young, eager. For myself, I'd like to assemble a department of specialists, who are congenial, but who will see areas of our work as their own. As we build toward specialization, and we must, there will be debate, but we must end by going strong in one or two or three areas, so that we may build library resources. I've been holding off this sort of decision making until we can talk it out together. There will be battles ahead, and we must present a united front where facing opposition. I think we are compatible and can be frank. I want you here....[38]

MacKirdy joined the faculty in July and attracted a group of others to come to Waterloo.

Ralph Stanton was particularly successful in recruiting for the University of Waterloo.[39] One of those whom he attracted was James Kalbfleisch, who came to Waterloo immediately after completing his undergraduate degree at the University of Toronto. Kalbfleisch, who later became professor of Mathematics, Dean of Mathematics, and ultimately Vice-President Academic and Provost, recalled Stanton's personal interest in choosing and wooing new faculty members. Stanton telephoned Kalbfleisch in Toronto, suggesting they meet, and although very interested, Kalbfleisch explained that he had arranged to see his fiancée, a student at the University of Western Ontario, and he had to catch the bus to London. Not to be deterred, Stanton said that he would happily drive him to London. Jim Kalbleisch joined Waterloo the following September. Newly married just before term began, Kalbfleisch mentioned to Stanton that he needed someone to fill in for the first few weeks of class. 'No problem,' said Stanton, 'I will teach them for you.' And so he did.[40] Stanton also brought senior scholars such as Kenneth Fryer from the Royal Military College in Kingston and Gerald Berman from the Illinois Institute of Technology in Chicago. He and Gerald Berman persuaded one of the University of Toronto's most talented mathematicians, William Tutte – who, years later was revealed as having worked at Bletchley Park during World War II as a successful code breaker – to come to Waterloo.[41]

Gerald and I went down to Toronto with the deliberate idea of stealing Bill Tutte. Tutte was not really appreciated at Toronto. He was only an Associate Professor after about 12 years and was probably the most creative mind on the Toronto faculty. Gerald and I knew him quite well. We relied on the fact that he was an old friend and also that we were good friends with Dorothy [Tutte]. Bill and Dorothy met hiking and they were both ardent hikers… So we met and talked to them in their apartment. We were talking at Bill but really to Dorothy because it was quite clear that one had only to persuade Dorothy. We offered him a good salary and a full professorship, and Bill came and never regretted it.[42]

Bill Tutte's work at Waterloo contributed to the university's predominance in a number of fields of Mathematics, including Graph Theory, Combinatorics and Optimization, and programs in Cryptography.

MATHEMATICS AND THE ARTS FACULTY

An interesting and unanticipated issue in the earlier relationship with Waterloo College and the separate creation of a Faculty of Arts at the University of Waterloo was the decision to locate the Department of Mathematics in the Faculty of Arts rather than in the Faculty of Science. Stanton liked to say that mathematics, and especially his area of numerical analysis, was "partly a science and partly an art." He taught his courses to students in Arts and Science and Engineering. This had not been a problem at the University of Toronto, where his Faculty was Arts and Science, and where engineering students regularly enrolled in his numerical analysis courses. At Waterloo College, however, Arts and Science were separate faculties.

With the Science Faculty, along with Engineering, moving to the University of Waterloo, Stanton had become Chairman of Mathematics at the University. At first, Stanton and the other mathematicians had identified themselves with the Science Faculty, especially since the University was still negotiating with Waterloo College about the future of Arts. "Since most of the [Mathematics] courses would be given in the Faculty of Science, and since the degree in Mathematics and Physics would be granted through the Faculty of Science, it would appear advisable that the Department should be located in that Faculty," he had reasoned.[43] Before the year was out, however, politics clearly came into play. In November 1959, Stanton informed President Hagey that, "In accordance with our recent conversation, I have consulted the members of the department as to whether they feel the Department of Mathematics should belong to the Faculty of Arts or the Faculty of

Science, within the University of Waterloo. The result of our discussions is that the Department of Mathematics should be in the Faculty of Arts of the University of Waterloo, but not in the Faculty of Arts of any affiliated, federated, or otherwise associated colleges."[44] Stanton later recalled, "When I came here I don't think it [the creation of a separate Faculty of Mathematics] was in the back of my mind, I was just intent on building up a good mathematics department, in the broadest sense of mathematics, including applied mathematics and numerical analysis. Then when the split with Waterloo College came, it was sort of agreed, I can't say whose idea it was, it was just sort of agreed as a consensus among President Hagey and the people in science and engineering, that it would be a good idea if mathematics was in the Arts Faculty at that time, simply because the Arts Faculty was almost nonexistent. We had a couple of people in English, like Al Dust, but basically, at the very beginning, the Department of Mathematics was the Arts Faculty."[45]

Mathematics was now separate from the Faculty of Science, whereas in other universities, science, and especially physics, tended to be predominate over mathematics. When the Physics and Mathematics building was completed in February 1960, E.W.R. Steacie, Chairman of the National Research Council, travelled to Waterloo to open the new building and quipped that it was interesting to see the name of Mathematics on a building: "It is not often that mathematics gets its name on the building. Usually the mathematician has to be content with some unwanted space in an attic and it is pleasant to see them get their due for once. I noticed, however, they haven't quite made it yet since the course in the calendar is Maths and Physics, but the building is Physics and Mathematics."[46] When he made his remarks, Steacie could not have anticipated the role that mathematics was destined to play at Waterloo.

From the beginning, the University of Waterloo benefited from Ralph Stanton's desire to make Mathematics a department second to none in the university; for his part, Stanton benefited from the University's competitive spirit and its recognition that Mathematics was not a discipline to behoused in an out-of-sight garret. For Mathematics to thrive, however, more was needed than a permissive atmosphere and talented professors. Students are the lifeblood of any university, and Stanton's personal reputation not only attracted such stellar students as Ron Mullin, Eric Manning, Gus German, and Jerry Lawless, each of whom would leave a permanent imprint on the University's future success, but Stanton, along with his colleague Ken Fryer, developed an aggressive and innovative recruitment program to attract the best mathematics students in Ontario. Travelling across the province, especially to newer schools in Northern Ontario, Stanton and Fryer showed the importance of Mathematics to schools and students alike. This tactic brought outstanding students to Waterloo and instilled a sense of loyalty to this new university, which had come to them. Equally successful was his support for a series of innovative Mathematics competitions which soon were nation-wide and made Waterloo and Mathematics co-terminus and from this, as students began arriving at Waterloo, Mathematics became almost a stand-alone discipline within the university.

Ralph Stanton steadily raised the profile of his discipline. It is not surprising, perhaps, that the first degree awarded by the University of Waterloo was an M.A. in Mathematics. Stanton continued to use his contacts with former students from the University of Toronto to recruit candidates for graduate studies in Mathematics, ensuring a coterie of gifted graduate students, many of whom were given teaching assignments while they continued their research. All of this placed Mathematics in the vanguard of the profession and secured a unique position for the department within the university. The timing and the opportunities for advancement came together, and Stanton seized them.

MATHEMATICS AND CO-OPERATIVE EDUCATION

At first, Ralph Stanton had been unconvinced about Co-operative education in Arts until the spring of 1962 when three insurance companies with head offices in Waterloo approached President Hagey with a novel idea. Writing on behalf of the insurance companies, Mutual Life, Dominion Life, and Equitable Life, T. R. Suttie, whose daughter, Wendy, was enrolled in Waterloo's Arts faculty, hoped to convince the university to consider extending its Co-operative education plan to include mathematics. As Suttie explained, "We would like to suggest [that] actuarial Mathematics would be particularly suitable for this approach, and to offer the full support of our companies."[47] Stanton took the opportunity, seeing the merit of co-operation with the insurance companies and believing that it would not disrupt the Mathematics program since it was possible to run both an honours mathematics program and a Co-operative option simultaneously.[48] Many mathematics graduates chose to enter the teaching profession and they preferred the regular program, but the Co-operative option opened a new professional dimension to those who sought other careers, and this was especially appealing once computer applications were linked to the Mathematics department.

In order to distance his department's plans from an earlier Co-operative education debate in other programs in Arts, Stanton stressed that his plans for Co-operative mathematics were in no way related to a general Arts Co-operative program. President Hagey could not have been more pleased. Hagey had long wanted to expand Waterloo's Co-operative program, but had met mixed views within the university and little support from industry. That Mathematics had been pursued by the insurance industry gave it a special cachet. Hagey proudly described this addition to Waterloo's Co-operative program to the province's Committee on University Affairs as an example of the relevance and value of Waterloo's educational initiatives. It added additional lustre to the Waterloo experiment. With little debate, the Arts Faculty Council moved its approval on January 14, 1964. A new era at Waterloo was about to begin.[49]

Set to commence in September 1964, the Co-op option in mathematics was a relatively simple matter – a reflection of Waterloo's burgeoning strength in applied areas of mathematics. There had been no need to create a new curriculum. The department simply offered the existing mathematics honours program on an alternating four-month basis. Although the majority of courses in the Arts Faculty were full-year courses – that is, one course for the fall and winter terms – by virtue of the service teaching provided to the Faculties of Science and Engineering, the Department of Mathematics had always offered some of its courses on a semester basis, making the transition to Co-operative education seamless. Stanton was convinced that the enrolment in the regular honours mathematics program would not decline, but rather that the heightened visibility of the Mathematics Department through Co-operative education would have only a positive overall effect.[50] Furthermore, this was not only an opportunity for actuarial mathematics students, but, with the increasing presence of computers in business, there was a growing demand for students who understood this application of mathematical principles. When the mathematics Co-operative option was announced to the public, twenty-nine insurance companies and corporations with computer facilities confirmed their participation in the new program.[51] And this was only the beginning!

The results exceeded everyone's expectations. The department had originally planned to accept only forty students into the program in 1964, but received so many qualified applicants that it decided to stretch its resources and take in one hundred. Stanton felt that mathematics could easily accommodate these additional sixty students. Additional staff, especially a director for the actuarial division, would have to be hired. (The appointment of C.F.A. Beaumont to this position was critical for the development of the Co-operative program in Mathematics and for the discipline's success at Waterloo.) Funds were also needed to launch a publicity campaign in high schools and to promote the merits of the program to industry. The department asked for a $125,000 grant from the government to pursue further development.[52] President Hagey was delighted to take the request for additional funds for the program to Queen's Park where, in the face of scepticism from other universities, he had long been touting the advantages of Co-operative education.[53]

A SEPARATE BUILDING, WHY NOT A SEPARATE FACULTY OF MATHEMATICS?

The rapid growth of Mathematics and the increasing demand for its courses led inevitably to the suggestion that there should be a separate building to house the Department of Mathematics, the new Computing Centre, space for the Co-ordination department, and even a Library for Engineering, Mathematics and Science. With a separate building, why not a separate Faculty of Mathematics? The relationship of Mathematics with the other departments in the Faculty of Arts was tenuous at best, but so much had happened at the University of Waterloo campus that the debates of the Evangelical Lutheran Synod seemed of no relevance to the place of Mathematics in the new University. The notion of a separate "organization" for Mathematics at Waterloo had been informally discussed from "time to time," but it was not until December 1964 that Stanton began to take the concept outside of his department. As the mathematics department grew and diversified, its administrative organization had been structured to mirror a faculty with the Chairman as its de facto dean. In an aside in a memorandum to Dean High regarding increased faculty allotments for the mathematics department, Stanton had been only half joking when he commented: "(Perhaps I should even say 'additions to a faculty [instead of department],' since mathematics is now really made up of many sub-departments such as pure mathematics, applied mathematics, computer science, actuarial mathematics, logic, statistics, etc.)"[54] Stanton also reminded Dean High that Mathematics had enough students to warrant the idea of a separate Faculty structure being considered, although he conceded that this was uncharted territory. Claiming the department's "reactions were almost uniformly very favourable," in April 1965 Stanton approached President Hagey with a plan for creating a Faculty of Mathematics. Wanting the launch of the new Faculty to coincide with the opening of the Mathematics and Computer building in 1967, Stanton conceded that he was attempting to create something without precedent. No other

university in North America had a Faculty of Mathematics, nor did the university have an established protocol for considering it. Seeking Hagey's recommendation on how to proceed was strategic for it brought the president into the loop and provided a sense of legitimacy to the entire process.[55] No sooner was Stanton's request public than a debate over it ignited, led by the members of the Science Faculty who vehemently objected to the suggestion that the mathematics department be allowed to pursue faculty status.

Science Dean W.A.E. McBryde and the heads of the science departments petitioned Hagey to have the entire proposal rejected on principle, arguing that "to split a university up into more isolated units than is absolutely necessary is contrary to the whole idea of a university, an idea which is even suggested by the name university." Not only was the proposed faculty perceived as a threat to university cohesiveness, but by virtue of offering a degree without precedent, it also risked damaging the credibility of the University of Waterloo. "The fact that no university has set one up is a clear indication that this is not regarded favourably even in larger institutions," they suggested. "We doubt if this university should pioneer in this development, in spite of the rather anomalous position of mathematics in relation to the existing faculties." McBryde also feared that allowing Mathematics to become a separate faculty would encourage other large departments to attempt the same, splintering the university even further.[56]

Stanton resented the implication that his proposal was rash or potentially dangerous, claiming instead that the idea had been given careful consideration, and since the prospective launch date was not for another two years, there was ample time to consider the options. He rejected concerns that smaller administrative groupings were contrary to the idea of a university. Instead, he suggested, they allowed for faculties to be more efficient. After all, Graduate Studies, with its seventeen departments, had been deemed too cumbersome; with fourteen departments to administer, why should the same not be said for Arts? Finally, Stanton felt that Science's aversion to "pioneering" was completely without foundation: "That anything new and unique should not be instituted, is surely an inappropriate argument here at the University of Waterloo."[57] It ran contrary to the whole spirit of Waterloo. This was the university, after all, that eight

years earlier had dared to launch a Co-operative education program in the face of concerted opposition from the other Ontario universities.

Douglas Wright, Dean of Engineering and friend, ally, and admirer of Ralph Stanton, supported him over Science's objections. Wright argued that there was already a fair amount of isolation in the Arts and Sciences and added: "I would suggest, albeit tentatively, that this university and most others would better serve their intended functions if patterns of organization reflected the needs of students more than the parochial interests of departments and faculty." He also recognized that as the university continued to grow, new patterns of organization would need to be put in place.[58] In reality, like Stanton, Wright was restless and anxious to see Waterloo move beyond conventional boundaries. Would this be the only new faculty to be created at Waterloo? Three years later, the Arts Faculty would again be riven when a Faculty of Environmental Science was established. But Mathematics had set the precedent. Why not another new faculty?[59]

Neither the Dean of Arts nor any of the faculty members in Arts had engaged in the early debate about creating a Faculty of Mathematics. President Hagey was keen to go forward, but was also cautious. On May 20, he announced that Mathematics would be allowed to pursue its idea; but first, a committee needed to be established by the Arts Faculty Council to discuss the plan, and because Mathematics provided service teaching for Engineering and Science, both of those faculties needed to be consulted as well.[60] Thus encouraged, Stanton turned his energies to canvassing support for the idea of a Faculty of Mathematics. Ever the back room politician and master strategist, Ralph Stanton was in his element. In some ways, he liked this best of all.

From Stanton's point of view, mathematics was neither a science nor an art, but a combination of each, and this was the root of the problem. "Mathematical programs should be set, administered, and controlled by mathematicians," he said, "and to this end uniting the seven hundred mathematics students under one administrative centre was the most logical course of action."[61] Stanton concluded that Arts had no strong feeling against the idea of a Mathematics Faculty, but that additional consideration was needed before the proposal could be endorsed.[62] An ad hoc committee was established, as well as a committee of Arts department heads to investigate the plan in greater depth.[63] Engineering posed no threat; Wright and the members of his Faculty were favourably disposed to the principle of a new Faculty.[64] Stanton and Wright had often been allies, and they would be so again. The meeting with McBryde and the science department heads was not nearly so successful. The majority of the Science Faculty rejected the proposal for a separate faculty and the new degree in Mathematics that would be created. If Stanton merely wanted more administrative control, they suggested, why not divide the Faculty of Arts into three schools – Humanities, Social Sciences, and Mathematics?[65] The Arts Faculty cautiously considered Stanton's proposal. Many were happy to see Mathematics out of their way, since by virtue of its size and the forcefulness of its personalities, mathematics had dominated the faculty council, and this irritated many faculty members. According to Paul Cornell, the departure of mathematics had the potential to actually be a good thing for the Arts Faculty as a whole.[66]

Perhaps not surprisingly, Psychology Department Chairman Richard Walters, whom Stanton had encouraged to come to Waterloo, moved at the Arts Faculty Council meeting on November 23, 1965, that "the petition of the department of Mathematics for the establishment of a Faculty of Mathematics be sent to the Senate Committee on University Academic Organization." The motion was carried.[67] As legend has it, Stanton was going to have his way on this matter and his "ducks" were lined up in a row. Peter Ponzo, a young mathematics professor, described how the entire Mathematics Department was rounded up and marched into the amphitheatre where the crucial vote was to be held. "Ralph sat by himself, several rows from the back so that all his people could see him. There was a low groan from the other members of the Arts Faculty. When it came time to vote on the issue, Ralph raised his right hand. There was but a moment's pause, then every hand in the back rows rose in unison."[68]

No sooner was the first vote taken than Walters again stood before council to move that "the Arts Faculty Council supports the idea of the establishment of a Faculty of Mathematics." No vote was taken.[69] The matter was settled – or almost settled. At the next meeting of Faculty Council a secret ballot was held. Fifty members of the Arts Faculty voted in favour of the creation of a Faculty of Mathematics; thirty-five voted against the resolution and four abstained.[70] It was enough: Stanton had his endorsement. It was time to take the issue to Senate.

The Senate Committee on University Academic Organization first met to discuss the Mathematics Department's proposal in January 1966. The issues were not new. There were still grave concerns about the implications for unity within the university, admissions standards, the effect this would have on the affiliated colleges, the potential for other departments to petition for their own faculties, and the overall effects of the changes for the administration of the faculty.[71] One of the proposal's most ardent critics, the Dean of Science, was a member of the committee. (McBryde confided to Stanton that he knew Mathematics would carry the day, but that for the sake of his own Faculty he was obliged to push their case.) On March 7, 1966, on the strength of the Department of Mathematics draft constitution, Stanton's motion that "the Senate Committee on University Academic Organization recommend to Senate the establishment of a Faculty of Mathematics" carried.[72] Final approval came on April 28, 1966. Vice President Batke moved and Stanton seconded the motion at Senate to approve the establishment of a Faculty of Mathematics. The motion was carried.[73] Stanton had managed to do what no one anywhere else had even thought to try. He gave mathematics the visibility he felt the discipline had long been denied by many institutions of higher learning – he had created a Faculty of Mathematics.[74]

Released from his duties as Dean of Graduate Studies and armed with the Senate's approval, Stanton began to prepare the Mathematics Department for the transition year. The new Faculty would come into being on July 1, 1967, in time for the unofficial opening of the new Mathematics and Computer building, the largest building on Waterloo's campus. Unexpectedly, after nine years at the University of Waterloo, on July 19, 1966, Ralph Stanton announced to a stunned department that the president had granted him a leave of absence for the coming academic year. Kenneth Fryer was temporarily to assume the responsibilities of chair of the department.[75] Ultimately, the leave of absence became permanent, and Ralph Stanton did not return to the University of Waterloo. His departure was significant for the Faculty of Arts. Stanton was a strong leader at the Arts Faculty Council meetings. Though he used his influence to ensure the success of Mathematics, Stanton had also set a direction for the faculty. Within a year of Stanton's departure, Norman High resigned as Dean of Arts, suggesting that "the time is here for the University to have the opportunity of utilising new resources of energy and creativity that can come with new personnel in the office which I now occupy."[76] The creativity did continue at a rapid pace: it was announced that phase III of the campus development would begin immediately, highlighting another of the campus's landmark buildings, the Hagey Hall of the Humanities.

In a city such as Waterloo lacking a centre for the performing arts, the Humanities Theatre quickly became the major venue for cultural events, complementing the original Theatre of the Arts. Under the talented leadership of maestro Raffi Armenian, the Kitchener-Waterloo Symphony, which had acquired an international reputation for excellence, moved its concert series to the Humanities Theatre. Named after President Hagey, this new building was a fitting tribute to the man who had so energetically pushed and cajoled the community to support the University of Waterloo. It was equally fitting that, when the building was opened in 1970, the Hagey Lecture Series chose this occasion to identify its premier lecture series in the building honouring the university's former president.

In May 1956, Hagey had described his ideas for a possible university in Waterloo, as the "thinking that has been done in the interests of the future of Waterloo College Associate Faculties." The Board of Governors proposed to chart a radical course for the Associate Faculties. Although incorporated "primarily as a College of Science," the Associate Faculties was "at liberty to offer a large range of courses" and was actually the "beginning [of] a new university" – one that would play "an important role in the future continued development of our province and nation."[77]

Although the world had moved "into a technological era" which "radically changed the demand from industry for labour, technicians, and engineers," Hagey explained, technological education in Canada paid little attention to the humanities; yet as technicians assumed new levels of responsibility, this cultural background would be essential. Waterloo, he suggested, was in a position "to formulate a curriculum that combines science, technology and the humanities," setting a course that looked to the future rather than one that was based on past university precedents. Hagey and his colleagues felt confident they could do it, even if the older universities could not.[78] Fifty years later, one suspects, President Hagey would be pleased with the university that he had done so much to shape and the building that was named in his honour. In a report of St. Jerome's first year on the university campus, St. Jerome's Dean of Arts, Father John Finn, recalled his delight in the relationship with the University of Waterloo and with the other religious denominations who were in the process of establishing their colleges on the campus. President Hagey, Finn remarked, speaks of Waterloo being "an interdenominational rather than a denominational university." According to Father Finn, "One of the things that has become apparent during the course of the year is that there is a quite general positive determination to cultivate harmonious relations between College and College and between the Colleges and the faculties of the University." And, Finn concluded, "…what has taken place is all for the good…what has happened is [that] the citizens of a whole university city have begun to converse about the things of the spirit in a way that was not possible a very short time ago."[79]

At the University's inaugural Convocation, Chancellor Dana Porter, himself an Arts graduate from the University of Toronto, conferred the University's first degree on Ronald Mullin for his work in Mathematics. At Waterloo's second Convocation, the first students earning Bachelor's degrees were in Arts, graduating through St. Jerome's College.[80] The following year, at the third Convocation, the first three candidates for the Bachelor of Arts degree were all women who had attended St. Jerome's: Barbara Austin, Constance Boos, and Sandra Brenner. Not until the fourth Convocation, on Saturday, July 7, 1963 did the first Engineering students receive their degrees.

The presence of a Faculty of Arts and its Arts graduates was more than symbolic. They were, in fact, the University of Waterloo's first graduates, going on to distinguished careers in Canada and abroad. Graduates from these classes served their nation as diplomats, members of the judiciary, doctors, lawyers, and librarians; accountants, novelists, teachers, social workers, and scholars. Some became senior administrators at other universities, Deans, Vice-Presidents, and Principals; others returned to Waterloo as Principals and Associate Provosts; still others became Members of Parliament, Members of the Order of Canada and Fellows of the Royal Society. Their degrees and their education in the Faculty of Arts made a difference to their lives and to the nations they served.

From the beginning, President Hagey recognized that the relationship of the Faculty of Arts to the university was not a replica of what had developed at Western or Toronto. The four colleges added both

architectural and intellectual dimensions at the undergraduate and graduate levels and made Waterloo a more comprehensive and intellectually vibrant university. With a wide range of course offerings in fifteen different departments, from Anthropology and Sociology to Classical Studies and Religious Studies, from Drama and Speech Communication to Philosophy and Economics, the Faculty of Arts is the University of Waterloo's largest faculty. The Faculty of Arts also added a faculty-wide program of Applied Arts Co-operative studies in 1980, later in 2004 renamed Arts and Business. Conferences in Elizabethan Theatre, with links to the Stratford Shakespearean Festival, and a program in Rhetoric and Professional Writing in the English Department broaden the faculty's array of interests, while International Finance in Economics, and graduate programs in Global Governance and in International Development in concert with the Centre for International Governance Innovation, sponsored by the History, Economics, and Political Science departments continue to enrich the Arts Faculty's areas of strength. For more than two decades, Waterloo's School of Accountancy has provided a unique national focus to the Arts Faculty. International standing in the Psychology Department's areas of research, its extensive publication record, and the

quality of its graduates has set Waterloo's program apart from other Canadian universities. The strong place in the faculty of the study of other cultures and languages with innovative exchange programs –with the German Department in Mannheim, as well as the German Department's Centre for German Studies and the French Department's program in Nantes – provide added international dimensions for Waterloo's students quite apart from the international studies options in both the regular Arts stream and the Co-operative Arts and Business program. Programs in Fine and Performing Arts continue to enrich the University and the larger community. The separation of Geography and Planning from the Faculty of Arts to form the nucleus of Canada's first Faculty of Environmental Studies, while still maintaining a relationship with the Arts Faculty, exemplifies the

creative push and pull of Arts at Waterloo. No ordinary faculty, this; no ordinary university. From its controversial beginnings, the Faculty of Arts has established itself as a central part of the university's cultural and intellectual life.

Were he able to look back at Waterloo's Faculty of Arts, President Hagey would be delighted at the number of former Arts students who returned to Waterloo to contribute to the University's development as a centre for learning. Paul Beam, a member of the first class in Arts, joined the English department; Manfred Kuxdorf became a professor of German. Soon after, Sandra Burt, and later Andrew Cooper, joined the Department of Political Science, Emmanuel Carvalho returned to the Department of Economics, James Walker and John English became historians, and Henry Paetkau is President of Conrad Grebel University College. Lois Claxton serves as Secretary of the University. After some years at Glendon College, and a term as President of the Canadian Historical Association, Gail Cuthbert Brant became Principal of Renison College before being seconded to the University of Waterloo as Associate Vice-President, Academic and Interim Associate Vice-President Learning Resources and Innovation. Douglas Letson was President of St. Jerome's University before being awarded an honorary LLD from Waterloo in 2006. The trend of returning graduates continues with Cristina Vanin in Religious Studies, Brian Orend in Philosophy, Marlene Epp and Whitney Lackenbauer in History. Another Waterloo Arts graduate, Kenneth Lavigne is the University's Registrar and David Fransen is Associate Provost and Executive Director of the University's Institute for Quantum Computing. This list is fragmentary and incomplete and it continues to expand as the University moves ever forward. The names cited above are by no means an inclusive list; rather, they serve as an indication of the role of the Arts Faculty and its graduates from the pioneering days at Waterloo to the present, helping to lead their university and its students into the next half century and beyond.

CHAPTER THREE

A remarkable decade 1957 - 1967

On the eve of the University's tenth anniversary, Ira Needles, Chair of the Board of Governors since the university's inception and the university's second Chancellor, took a moment to talk to the graduating students.[1]

At a time such as this [he began], I hope that I may be pardoned for reminiscing about the satisfaction that I have had in watching and taking part in the growth and development of the University of Waterloo.

It seems only a few short years since I attended a meeting [in 1956, to consider the needs of the community for higher education] …Little did we think at that time that we were talking about an institution which within a period of about ten years would be the third largest university in Ontario with an enrolment in excess of many of the Universities which at that time were well established.

How well does anyone tonight still remember the prefabricated building on a rented car-parking lot which was our only facility when our first 74 students enrolled? Clearly their courage matched ours when one remembers that no final degree could then be promised.

Brick and mortar in sizeable quantities are essential facilities for modern universities, but it is primarily people rather than buildings that make a university a great university…

These physical developments are interesting, but the proven ability of the University to attract well qualified faculty and staff members is much more impressive and meaningful to me…

It has been a source of satisfaction to me personally as well as to the members of our Board of Governors to find that the pioneering spirit which was shown during the first few years of the University's existence has continued. The co-operative timetable has been adopted by departments in our other undergraduate faculties as well as by one department in our graduate faculty…[And] A similar pioneering spirit has been evident during the life of the University in many ways beyond that of the departments in which co-operative programs are offered. This spirit has made possible a development of strong academic departments in the humanities, sciences, the social sciences, and other areas of studies.

Within a period of ten years this university has probably achieved as many firsts in higher education as have been achieved by any other university in Ontario, or even Canada. However, I hasten to state that simply doing something for the first time is not necessarily good. Our feeling of pride in our "firsts" comes from a knowledge that these achievements either have proved or are proving to be of a high standard and to be fulfilling a useful purpose in the country's academic, social, and industrial growth.

1967 will be the University's decennial year. All those who are associated with the University, including its students, may well feel proud of that which has been achieved in the first ten years. In 1957 the University accepted what appeared to be an impossible challenge. It has now proved its ability to meet that challenge. Conceivably the challenge of the next ten years may be equally as great in spite of the sound foundation that has been provided. I had confidence in the ability of the people who associated themselves with us in 1957 to succeed. I have equally as much confidence that ways will be found to do the things which the University considers desirable and needed during the next ten years. I have developed an interest in this University which exceeds that which I have had in any enterprise in which I have participated. I look forward with a great deal of pleasure to watching the University of Waterloo continue its progress toward becoming an even finer and greater university. I assure you that my interest in it will continue and that wherever possible I will make myself available for doing all that is within my power to help this institution achieve its objectives both for now and in the future.

1957 was a year not likely to be forgotten by the University of Waterloo's students or by the City of Waterloo. One hundred years earlier on January 1, 1857 local residents had celebrated the inauguration of their village, with great excitement as a small cannon, cast at Jacob Bricker's foundry, boomed its message that Waterloo had come of age – or so they thought then. In that previous century, the Village and later the Town of Waterloo had grown slowly and Jacob Bricker's cannon continued to celebrate festive occasions until, after several serious accidents, the cannon was retired to Waterloo Park. In 1948, when Waterloo attained cityhood, its boundaries remained those of its incorporation as a village. With the exception of the outbursts from the cannon, city life seemed little changed from the previous 100 years. The arrival of so many new students in 1957 and the

establishment of a new university-in-the-making would end that. Like all students, they brought a unique liveliness, and their need to identify themselves and their traditions brought national attention to Waterloo.

In Ottawa, in 1957, Prime Minister Louis St. Laurent was considering an important speech to the university presidents of Canada. As leader of Canada's governing party, in power more or less since the days of Wilfrid Laurier, in anticipation of a federal election, he had good news for them. Arising from the recommendations of the Massey Report was the idea of a Canada Council to support the creative arts. St. Laurent wanted to encourage the creation of a Canadian culture, but he had serious reservations about the artistic community. Universities, on the other hand, were popular in the public mind. They had done great things in the war and they had done even more for veterans returning home from overseas service – since education was a provincial responsibility, all of this with very little financial assistance from his government. St. Laurent's announcement of $100 million to create a Canada Council was accompanied by a fund of $60 million for universities to aid in rebuilding post-secondary education.

The newly announced Co-operative program at Waterloo, with three months in the classroom alternating with three months in the workplace, seemed appropriate to the time. Admission to the pre-engineering program, as it was then called, did not depend on the achievement of Grade 13 standing, but was determined by an eight-hour examination designed to measure students' aptitude. The intention was clearly to appeal to students with an interest in science and engineering, but who had not always been successful in the traditional high school curriculum. The three-month work term also allowed students from modest means to finance their education, and three months was much less of a burden than the traditional eight-month program in place at other Canadian universities. It was a risk worth taking: a chance for university education for students who were willing to try something new and different.

Shortages of trained technicians and engineers in Canada were acute and the pressures of Cold War competition were mounting, creating a crisis in engineering education. *The Globe and Mail* published an editorial during the summer of 1956 arguing that to be competitive in the increasingly technical and industrial world, Canada needed to educate another 150,000 engineers.[2] Worried Canadian business leaders met at St. Andrews-by-the-Sea, New Brunswick in September 1956 to discuss the state of engineering in Canada at a National Conference on Engineering, Scientific and Technical Manpower.[3] Two weeks before the Conference in New Brunswick, at a meeting of the Kitchener-Waterloo Rotary Club,[4] Ira Needles announced Waterloo College Associate Faculties' plan to initiate the idea of Co-operative education, explaining that in this kind of program, "industry cooperates with the college in training the student who spends one quarter of a year in college and the next quarter period of training in industry." Success in both terms was necessary for continuation in the program.[5]

The opportunity to 'make something happen' had fuelled Gerald Hagey's decision to accept the presidency of Waterloo College, and the sense of urgency expressed in Needles' remarks and at the New Brunswick meetings provided the means to do so. The timing of the Waterloo Co-operative education program was also critical to its success. The success of the Soviet launch of Sputnik the following year on October 4, 1957 and the failure of the United States and the West to adequately respond to the first man-made satellite confirmed many of the fears expressed during the previous few years. In discussing the University of Toronto's response to the launch of the Sputnik, Martin L. Friedland remarked that "[I]t was widely felt [that the West] was losing its pre-eminence in Science and Technology. [Toronto President Claude] Bissell recorded the despair at the time: 'The Russian satellite has created a general gloom, and now the dismal failure of the first American attempt to launch a counter-Sputnik has intensified the gloom."[6] Sputnik alone did not cause the crisis in engineering education that was already widespread by 1957, but it did concentrate popular attention on the urgent need for the expansion of education programs in general, and engineering specifically.[7] This provided a unique opportunity for Waterloo College Associate Faculties.

DEFINING CO-OPERATIVE EDUCATION

The Co-operative program expressed Hagey's sense of outreach to the community and Needles' belief that too many 'young men' were not being given an opportunity to attend university and when combined with a chance visit to Waterloo College by the Principal of the Provincial Institute of Trades, C.L. Emery, in the summer of 1956 it provided a form to the still inchoate ideas of what was intended to be a Science Faculty.[8] From this arose the idea of Co-operative education as the founding principle of a program in Applied Science, rather than in Science, and the next step was to find the faculty members to implement the program. After the June 1956 Board of Governors meeting, Emery became the Planning Engineer and then Principal of the Co-operative Applied Science Course.[9] Together, Emery and Hagey recruited Ron Bowman (to head the Department of Applied Physics), Ron Davies, and Don MacPherson from industry, Arthur Cowan, a Physicist at the National Research Council in Ottawa, Ted Batke from Dupont (for Chemical Engineering), and Ralph Stanton from the University of Toronto as Chairman of the Department of Mathematics. With this, the core faculty members were in place.[10]

One of their first steps was to reject the insistence of the University of Western Ontario, with which Waterloo College's Arts program was affiliated, that it could dictate the development of Engineering at the Waterloo College Associate Faculties. This long and complicated debate with the President of the University of Western Ontario described elsewhere, nearly ended the Associate Faculties' aspirations before they began.[11] The committee studied a number of possible engineering programs, including those offered at the Massachusetts Institute of Technology, and partly to assert their independence from the University of Western Ontario, the first courses were modelled on those taught at the University of Toronto. Not content to remain in the shadow of Toronto's orthodoxy, however, Waterloo's reputation as a leading university would be earned by developing a program of Co-operative education, and by creating a new engineering curriculum.

IRA NEEDLES AND WATERLOO

Ira Needles, Chair of the Board of Governors and President of B.F. Goodrich Canada, was part of the remarkable group of business leaders summoned to Ottawa during the World War II, who volunteered their business experience to the Canadian war effort. Needles' time in Ottawa had a profound effect on him and on his generation of industrial leaders. Important friendships were established, a sense of urgency and a belief in the destiny of the Canadian nation became a fixed part of their resolve to build a better future for their children. Needles' daughter, Lenora, fondly remembers visiting her father in Ottawa and dancing with him in the ballroom of the Chateau Laurier, which provided a moment of respite from the years of war as well as a personal glimpse of this sometimes-imposing business leader.[12] Needles once remarked that he always felt discouraged when his children's friends came by his home and had no idea of the possibilities that education offered. These feelings and these attitudes were an essential part of the momentum that drove him to support the Co-operative plan for education at Waterloo.

A no-nonsense business leader determined to move university education into the modern age, Ira Needles brought a unique background to developing what he called "the Waterloo Plan." As a young man, he had attended Coe College in Cedar Rapids, Iowa where he was captain of the football team. In 1915, he graduated from Northwestern University in Chicago, but remained for a year when the Dean of Commerce asked him to organize a bureau of employment for the University and to call upon employment managers in Chicago to advise them about students available for work. What an opportunity this was for Ira Needles. For one thing, he learned that, "If I had the right handle on my name – the manager of the Bureau of Employment for Northwestern University – doors opened almost magically… I would call people in top positions in the

major business organizations in Chicago, ask for an appointment for interviews, tell them why I wanted to see them, and I had no difficulty whatever in making these contacts. In fact it wasn't long before we had so many job openings listed that we couldn't send enough people to interview all of them. Out of this I learned a valuable lesson: the higher in business a man is, the more readily he is willing to see you if you have something really worthwhile to talk about. The university was the name that opened the door."[13] With his sleeves rolled up, Ira Needles was ready to do the same thing at Waterloo. When he retired from B.F. Goodrich in 1960, he moved to an office on the campus and began making more phone calls. This time he had the title: former President of B.F. Goodrich Canada and Chairman of the Board of Governors of the University of Waterloo.

To ensure that Co-operative education would be a success, he asked other business leaders to hire Waterloo's students, and he sought their help in encouraging their friends to do so as well as to assist him in raising funds on behalf of the Co-operative program. When the university planned its first fundraising campaign in 1957, Needles and President Hagey were advised that to launch a fund raising drive for the Associate Faculties' project would be "to invite a failure."[14] Brakeley and Company, professional fundraisers, conducted confidential interviews with industrialists and businessmen, as well as educators and the general public, and those whom they interviewed unanimously expressed "an uncertainty as to the [ability of the]Associate Faculty [sic] and its board of governors to carry through the plan as they understand it."[15] Furthermore, the acceptance and standing of graduates of the eventual university was also in doubt and severely limited the likelihood of success of a fundraising campaign.[16] They had not counted on Ira Needles. He and Hagey surged forward; failure and retreat were not part of their lexicon as they set out to raise $1.25 million. Brakeleys was right about one thing though, the fundraising campaign was neither simple nor easy. "I wore my shoe leather to the uppers calling on people to support the idea of a new university," Needles recalled. In order to persuade people to serve on the fundraising committee, Hagey added, "We had to invite five or six people in order to get one. People were interested in our story, but when I came to associating their names with the project, they wanted to wait until there was greater assurance of reaching our objective."[17]

As a new university that was still merely an idea, the fundraising committee faced an unusual list of difficulties. There were no alumni, traditionally a source of cash and canvassers. Furthermore, in 1957 there were no permanent buildings, no academic traditions; nor was there a football team, or a school song or banner. As it turned out, few donors gave more than $10,000. Needles, Hagey, and a group of committed volunteers, however, raised over $1 million – enough to convince the government of Ontario of the community's backing for the university. The number of small donations was significant – it was a sign of the community's support as much as it was an indication that Kitchener and Waterloo were still relatively small urban centers in the midst of southwestern Ontario. In response to this initiative, the government of Leslie Frost, itself a product of small-town Ontario, granted $8 million to the Associate Faculties in support of their program.[18]

Five years later, in 1962, the University of Waterloo embarked on its second fundraising campaign, hoping to raise $3 million. How things had changed. Waterloo's Co-operative Engineering program had made its imprint. This was a university different from the others, to be sure, but one that met a unique national need. As Gordon McCaffrey explained in a magazine for senior Canadian management, "When the University of Waterloo decided to launch its present $3 million Canadian Fund for expansion – i.e., a door- knocking appeal to business and industry – Chairman of the Board of Governors Ira G. Needles first directed his personal charm and the single-minded persuasiveness to the job of rounding up a team of captains who hobnob with the top brass of just about every company of consequence from Windsor to Montréal."[19] Needles mused, "Four years ago, a lot of people I asked wondered whether they should work for the University. Now they believe Waterloo is doing a job that needs to be done. They want to help." In addition to personal support for Needles, many business leaders were strongly committed to the university's Co-operative engineering program. "This is a unique method of teaching," one business executive explained. "It gives the students maturity and experience. And it enables many who couldn't otherwise enroll to pay their own way." The thirty-member Industrial Advisory Board, which was comprised of delegates from companies interested in engineering education and had been meeting at Waterloo twice a year "to present

industries' point of view on the programming of the co-operative education course," actively supported the new fundraising campaign. When the campaign began, forty-five presidents and vice-presidents of Canadian companies canvassed on behalf of the University and interest in the Waterloo program resulted in feature articles in leading newspapers and magazines across Canada.

The "Canadian Fund to Expand the University of Waterloo" speaks to us of the time and place that was Waterloo in 1962. As it explained, "The space-age brings new knowledge and new challenges with such bewildering speed that traditional university teaching methods cannot always keep pace. To keep education in step with our times our universities have to be prepared to pioneer and innovate as well as to preserve the invaluable heritage of the past. And the University of Waterloo's precedent-setting experiment in co-operative education proved that the new can be successfully blended with the traditional to meet today's needs. It demonstrates alertness and a fresh approach that augurs equally well for new teaching ventures in other fields. It is … education in tune with Canadian times."[20] In 2007 the University of Waterloo's fund-raising target is $350 million and two months before the celebration of the University's 50th anniversary, following an extremely rigorous competition, the Canadian Foundation for Innovation announced a $33 million grant to Waterloo- the largest amount awarded to any Canadian university.

Another local business leader, Carl Pollock, would have been delighted by the University's success in 2007. As the Board Chair who succeeded Needles when he was appointed Chancellor, Pollock had taken up the cause of the University of Waterloo with a passion. The minutes of the Advisory Council on University Affairs record a stirring debate between him and former Ontario Premier Leslie Frost, when Pollock accompanied President Hagey to petition the Ontario government for increased financial support for Waterloo. With a very tight provincial budget, Frost hesitated to grant additional funds to Waterloo. In the minutes of debate that followed, Pollock is recorded as saying:

You've shown us the problem [i.e. a limited budget], but we are here to present the University of Waterloo arguments. And the University of Waterloo merits special attention. It has developed an excellent program in engineering. And Canada depends on manufacturers. Manufacturers appreciate [that] Waterloo [is] rendering first-class service…[As a strong Canadian nationalist, Pollock pressed Frost for support for Waterloo when he noted that] The Americans have for many years thought of Canada as an extension of their market. For them our exports are merely raw material. But our manufacturers now see America as an extension of their market. Therefore we have seen our exports double. If we are to do the job, we need trained university graduates. Waterloo has responded to a need and therefore deserves attention.

Frost: You're still saying you want all this money.

Pollock: If manufacturers produce, taxes will go up.

Frost: Will you [the Canadian manufacturers] do this? We agreed to give you $3 million for three years…Send us in by next week the priorities you want. There may be something under the Christmas tree for you.[21]

If given an opportunity, many believe that Canada could compete with the United States and if given a chance, so could their universities. Leslie Frost and his successor as Prime Minister of Ontario, John Robarts, agreed. They may have been influenced by Dana Porter, their former cabinet colleague, and the former Treasurer of Ontario, now Chief Justice who also served as the Chancellor of the University of Waterloo. Proudly standing next to Prime Minister Robarts at the opening of Waterloo's Engineering building on April 12, 1962, Porter confessed that he felt a "fatherly interest" in the University of Waterloo. "It was during the time that I was Treasurer and Co-ordinator of Higher Education for the Province," he said, "that representatives from this university first informed me about their vision of a co-operative engineering course…It was the co-operative part of their planning that mainly interested me and caused me to support their request for provincial aid."[22] Along with Hagey and Needles, Dana Porter was responsible for Waterloo's early public success and over the next decade the government of John Robarts saw Waterloo emerge as one of Ontario's leading universities. Dana Porter's "interest in Waterloo" was rewarded.

BUILDING A PROGRAM IN CO-OPERATIVE EDUCATION:
IN THE DOMINION'S INTEREST

When Waterloo first announced the idea for a Co-operative program, Canadian industries enthusiastically embraced the concept, hiring Waterloo's students, featuring them in trade magazines, and declaring that Waterloo's Co-operative Engineering program was in the "Dominion's" interest, and that it fulfilled a national purpose. High praise was this, giving Waterloo a cachet and a reputation beyond what it had done on its own.

The dedication of the students who enrolled in Co-operative education and the first coordinators who took the university's ideas to their colleagues in industry played a vital part in the program's success. Hand-picked by A.S. Barber, the first Director of Co-ordination and Placement, the co-ordinators were professional engineers who knew the field and knew their students. They also knew many of the employers and took a hands-on role in developing Co-operative education. A.S. Barber had participated in the Co-op program at the General Motors Institute in Flint Michigan, now Kettering University, and he firmly believed that Co-operative education was more than job training. He made it a condition that companies participating in the Waterloo program assume a role in the education of the students. The co-ordinators recall the esprit de corps that he created, as well as his strong belief in what the university was trying to achieve. One of the early coordinators, Lloyd Jones, has provided a memoir that captures the unique relationship that existed among the coordinators, the employers, and the students. As Jones explained,

When I started at the University, I knew, personally, every engineer in Canada in the electric motor industry...most of them in the appliance industry and the aircraft industry. And the air conditioning industry. I had contacts with these people. Engineers would come up from Montreal to interview students, [and say] "Lloyd, what are you doing around here?"... And I knew them on a first-name basis, because I had travelled from Drummondville, Quebec to Winnipeg, and I knew most of the engineers in those industries. After only a short time, I could phone....Bell Telephone, Ontario Hydro, a lot of other companies...[and say] "I've got a live one!" [They'd say] "Okay, send him up!" And the student would sit there and say, "If you can find me a job that easy, why do I take interviews?" "Well, because they're good for you!"[23]

With Co-operative education as a distinguishing feature, Hagey hoped to promote Waterloo as an alternative to other Canadian universities. He gave a great deal of latitude to experiment with new ideas, and to execute different approaches to educational reform.

DEFINING CO-OPERATIVE EDUCATION
THE WRIGHT STUFF

Douglas Wright's arrival in 1958 as Chairman of Civil Engineering, then as Acting Dean of Engineering and for the next seven years Dean of Engineering, established Waterloo as a leading engineering school soon to have Canada's largest undergraduate enrolment. At the age of 31, Douglas Wright was the youngest Dean of Engineering in Canada, and he brought the excitement and vigour of someone so young along with an intellectual vitality and a commitment to change the practice of engineering well beyond his years. Wright had attended the University of Toronto in the years immediately after World War II when the campus was still at Ajax, Ontario, and he retained the restless spirit that had accompanied that class of engineering students, frustrated with the old ways of doing things and anxious to see Canada move forward. He had done post-graduate work at Illinois and at the University of Cambridge in England before joining the Faculty of Engineering at Queen's University and as a consultant he had witnessed firsthand new ways of engineering practice.

Impatient with the difficulty of implementing change in Engineering at Queen's, Wright agreed to visit Waterloo and was immediately caught up in its excitement and in the possibility of developing an Engineering school that would be modern in practice and relevant in its application of ideas to Canadian society. As he left behind the traditions of Queen's for Waterloo in the fall of 1958, Douglas Wright believed that engineering at Waterloo was essentially a blank slate, bound neither by a traditional curriculum nor an entrenched professorial staff. Waterloo was also open to a modern approach to curriculum development. For one thing, Ralph Stanton, Chairman of the Department of Mathematics, was offering numerical analysis as a key component of the engineering program. In Wright's judgement this distinguished the Waterloo program because nowhere else in Canada were universities instructing engineering students in finite mathematics: "Up to that time, Engineering had no rigorous analysis of real problems… [It was] just too bloody difficult," he recalled. "The real world is irregular and the only solutions were for regular situations." Traditional engineering analysis, he said, was extremely pragmatic: it was "safe to interpolate but very unsafe to extrapolate."[24] Wright believed that the key to resolving this problem was in finite mathematics and numerical analysis, both of which he had studied in graduate school, but was not an area that most Canadian universities were teaching to undergraduates.

The immediate importance of Wright's appointment was that it relieved Bruce Kelley of the deanship of the Faculty of Science and Engineering and created a separate Faculty of Engineering. Because the Faculty was so small, its administration was relatively simple and informal, but there was a great deal of enthusiasm regarding its future. Surprisingly, Wright had some doubt about whether or not he was the correct choice as Dean. "It should perhaps first be noted," he wrote, "that I was very surprised when this new appointment was suggested. I naturally shared with everyone at Waterloo the sense of need and urgency associated with our many problems in this time of great change. Needless to say, I was gratified by this indication of confidence in my ability to serve in such a position. On the other hand, however, I

feel that there is certain wastefulness in putting a person with years of special technical training into an administrative post, and I for one would never apply for such a position."[25] The others never had any second thoughts.

Wright's continuing interest in research influenced his priorities for the new Faculty, and the commitment to research also set the program at Waterloo apart from some other universities, where the practice of serving as consulting engineers often replaced academic research.[26] Aiding Wright considerably was Hagey's decision to approach the development of Waterloo differently from other universities. One historian writing of this era has suggested that "throughout the 1950s, university presidents argued that expansion should occur only within the abilities of the traditional system of curriculum and culture to absorb the new students."[27] Fear that the rapid expansion of 'multiversities' would reduce the quality of post-secondary education and threaten the stability of the universities was commonplace. By contrast, Hagey was anxious to explore alternative approaches to education and the University of Waterloo offered a new concept in instruction. Hagey and Douglas Wright agreed that new approaches could contribute to the educational system and that earlier traditions, while valuable, should not be used to restrict innovation at Waterloo.

"Such success as has already been achieved at Waterloo in the engineering course," Wright suggested, "must be primarily attributed to the novelty and the readily apparent features of the Co-operative pattern." He was quick to note, however, "In the long run, the real success of the Waterloo Co-operative engineering course must be evaluated in terms of total educational accomplishment – reflecting both the quality of the academic achievement and the real contribution of co-operative industrial experience in the educational process."[28] The acceptance of Waterloo's program was evident in 1963 when engineering enrolment in other Canadian universities began to decline and Waterloo's expanded, in no small part due to the success that "the

Co-operative program is playing in offsetting this trend and in attracting students to the engineering profession."[29]

It is not easy to evaluate the early work placements of students in the Co-operative program. Some students were highly complimentary of their experience and after graduation continued working with the companies in which they had been co-op students. Others had less positive experiences. The first Director, A.S. Barber, however, was particularly pleased when students suggested that the Co-op experience was equivalent to "taking another university course" while also acquiring a formal engineering education. However, Barber recognized that there were problems that needed to be sorted out. He worried that, "a significant number of employers are losing sight of the fact that the co-op plan is a method of education and not a method of recruitment." "Some co-op companies," he said, "have been greatly disturbed at losing their future students to non-co-operating companies at graduation and have suggested a preferential treatment." Students complained that some work programs were poorly planned or that students were used to cover unattractive and undesirable jobs and the levels of responsibility were below their abilities, while increases in wages did not follow their progress through the undergraduate period. Some of these complaints are inherent and remain as commonplace in 2007 as they were in 1957.

These were inevitable teething problems. No one mentioned that without the co-operation of labour unions, the concept of Co-operative education might never have succeeded; but that, too, is part of the success of this concept when Waterloo first introduced it in the Canadian context. As Co-operative education expanded beyond traditional engineering fields, which had often been considered as part of the professional background and outside of the areas of union organization, organized labour's acceptance of Waterloo's program was increasingly important, and they, too, saw their support of Co-op as in "the Dominion's interest."

In the early years, the suggestion of adding a conventional engineering program in tandem with the existing Co-operative program was also mooted, but when it was proposed in 1964 the Engineering Faculty Council strongly opposed it, stating that, "It was generally agreed that the enviable reputation of our engineering program has been largely due to the co-operative plan and… it would be a serious mistake to take the risk of damaging that reputation by introducing a conventional program."[30]

An unexpected consequence of the success of the Co-operative program was its attraction for international students, which posed new problems for the University and for the companies that employed Co-op students. Many Canadian companies, Barber explained, were not interested in taking foreign students who "would not be staying with their company, and because when they do go back [to their home countries] they become a disrupting influence if they go to branch plants."[31] He added that, "Companies who do not have overseas affiliations are basically looking for future employees who have management potential. While it must be agreed that this may or may not develop in any students, the odds are strongly against the selection of foreign students." The director worried about the consequences and admitted, "to save embarrassment on the part of the companies, we do not schedule these [international] students for regular interviews, but rather make individual placements which are most time-consuming… in some instances, the students feel like they are being discriminated against by us when we do not permit them to accept interviews. Again, I would repeat that this is to save embarrassment on the part of the companies. I am of the opinion that overseas students should be channelled to conventional courses and that we should limit our enrolment of them to a very minimal number."[32]

Dean Wright was sympathetic to Barber's concern about overseas students, and he had taken steps to limit their admission to the program. Wright worried about overseas students who saw the Co-operative engineering courses merely as a device to secure a university education at no cost.[33] "This," Wright said, "would be opposing the intentions of co-op employers." Following this discussion, Visa students were not admitted to the Co-operative program until the presidency of David Johnston reversed this practice and Waterloo began to aggressively recruit international students and to find work placements for them in Canada and in companies abroad. This was a necessary extension of the University's decision to take a greater role in the international community and to reinvent the place of Co-operative education at the University of Waterloo. It was also a recognition that the world had changed and that to be successful, Waterloo must be ranked not just among the best universities in Canada, but among the best in the world.

MORE ADJUSTMENTS TO CO-OPERATIVE EDUCATION

With no time for debate, Waterloo had originally adopted its alternating work-study schedule from a pre-existing American template of four three-month semesters for each academic year. Students were admitted in July, October, and January. This presented unexpected problems in the Canadian academic system.[34] Not only had no other Canadian university adopted such a schedule, but within Waterloo the other two faculties, Arts and Science, organized their programs and curricula along the standard academic year of four-month terms consistent with the requirements of the Ontario College of Education and other professional associations. In June 1960, Dean Wright recommended that Engineering abandon the four-semester sequence and convert to a three-semester system in which the fall and winter terms would be made to coincide with the two terms in Arts and Science. First year enrolment would take place entirely in the fall, with the class dividing in two at the beginning of the winter term for alternating work and study terms.[35] This change would not significantly alter the Co-operative engineering program, and although the number of periods in industry would be reduced, the total time in industry would be reduced only slightly. The fall and winter terms would now be concurrent with the ordinary academic terms in the other university faculties, making service teaching and the ability to relate to those faculties more likely.[36]

When administrative delays within the university threatened to prevent the implementation of the new schedule,[37] Wright complained to President Hagey about administrative stagnation that was developing within the university. "[I]t has not been possible to make better progress on plans for the inception of a four-month semester program in engineering," he said, "because of the complete and utter lack of any sense of pressure (save personal conscience) amongst many people for economies of operations in the University."[38]

Wright was concerned that administrative deadlock would ultimately negate a unique opportunity for innovation and development. His memo had the desired effect. The university's administrative machinery moved with despatch and in September, Hagey endorsed changing the academic schedule to three four-month terms.[39] In October, the three faculty councils of the university, Engineering, Arts, and Science, accepted the change of the engineering schedule[40], and in November, the Senate and the Board of Governors passed the change. Although only a technical issue, these amendments to the Waterloo Plan suggest a university where change was accommodated and where precedents weighed lightly. Pragmatic review and problem solving were at the heart of an engineer's training, and as such, they were at the heart of Waterloo's tradition. Hagey himself subscribed to this philosophy, noting, "We do not yet have many of the intolerable burdens that precedents have imposed on most other universities."[41]

PRE-ENGINEERING?

Along with these changes, one of Hagey's and Needles' prized initiatives, the pre-engineering option, also came up for review. Pre-engineering was essentially a Grade 13 equivalency course designed to prepare students for future engineering and technical training; thus, its curriculum was derived from high school content plus advanced mathematics. As the Faculty of Engineering grew in size and as the engineering curriculum became more complex, problems with pre-engineering demanded increasing attention. It had became a pressing concern in 1960 when the Coordination Department, responsible for managing Co-operative education, expressed concerns about the negative impact of pre-engineering's high failure rate on the Co-operative program. The very success of Co-operative education and its acceptance by more than 200 Canadian companies, with others forming a waiting list for students, had raised the bar for admission standards to the University of Waterloo. Visits to Ontario's high schools by engineering faculty members telling of the success of the university and of the value of Co-op placements led to a surge of highly qualified applicants. Once again, Waterloo had broken another barrier, as previously universities had drawn primarily from their local counties

and high school liaison was deemed unnecessary and unseemly. Waterloo's students came from across the province and across Canada. This, too, was novel for such a new university.

In the beginning, Gerry Hagey's dream was to attract young men who had dropped out of high school. For them, Co-operative education and the preliminary year program made their successful entry into university possible. Almost immediately, however, the success of Co-operative education in attracting so many top students made the idea of a preliminary program questionable. And then there was the concern of Ralph Stanton, who worried that the high failure rate of the pre-engineering program was having a negative effect on Waterloo's reputation with co-operating companies.[42] The problem was so bad, Stanton said, and the effects so damaging that he recommended that the Department of Coordination, the University's liaison with Industry, no longer attempt to place pre-engineering students in work terms and that students not be placed on an engineering work term until the completion of the first semester of the first engineering year. In some ways the existence of pre-engineering threatened both the academic reputation of the University and the success of the Co-operative program. The Director of the Department of Coordination and Placement, A.S. Barber, reported that several companies which had employed students from the pre-engineering program had dropped out of the Co-operative education program entirely or had asked that only students with Grade 13 be placed with them.[43] To clarify the issue, he requested a study of the pre-engineering program classes of October 1958, January 1959, October 1959, and January 1960, to determine the success of the students in particular and of the program in general. If the study showed, as he expected, a high failure rate, then pre-engineering students should be obliged to wait a full academic year before they could participate in Co-op.[44]

The investigation and report fell upon Douglas Wright, and his review confirmed Stanton's and Barber's suspicions. Only 48% of the pre-engineering students were admitted to year 1 Engineering, and of these fewer than half passed the first year university exams. This dismal performance compromised the future success of the University of Waterloo's experiment with Co-operative education. Wright was quite blunt when he explained that, "The

disproportionally high failure rate in the preliminary year, as compared with other university years has been a great source of embarrassment to the cooperating companies and the coordination department. The poor experience that companies have had with students in the preliminary year has resulted in a significant number of companies withdrawing from the co-operative program to the detriment of the entire course. Data from the co-ordination department indicates that most of the companies that have withdrawn from the co-operative program have done so because of their experience with preliminary year students."[45]

Despite these findings, Wright was not eager to eliminate the pre-engineering year, believing that he could save it. The main problem of pre-engineering, he felt, was not the quality of the students, but the pacing of the program and the immediate combination of academic and work terms: "Many students are not given an adequate opportunity to profit from the special opportunities offered in the preliminary year because the academic requirement in this qualifying year for the engineering course must be covered at a very rapid rate with the present six-month academic year."[46] The removal of the pre-engineering option from the Co-operative schedule, in Wright's opinion, strengthened the program and the academic year could then be lengthened to a full seven and a half month schedule. This would dissuade marginal students, leaving only "those students who are, in fact capable of university work."[47] He also suggested the university limit the admission to 48 students, with preference going to those students who were unable to complete grade 13 in the conventional fashion. Wright's continuing support for the preliminary year and Hagey and Needles' belief in its societal role were enough for the Board of Governors to continue the program. By early March 1961, pre-engineering was no longer a part of the Co-operative plan, but it remained an integral part of the engineering program at Waterloo. None-the-less, its days were numbered.

Two years later the Academic Budgets and Financial Planning Committee concluded that the pre-engineering year had probably "lived out its usefulness" and recommended it be discontinued. This time the concern had to do with university funding. Students in the preliminary year were not counted in determining provincial grants

and the only income for the program came from tuition fees. As a result, revenue constituted only about 40% of its total effective cost.[48] When word leaked out about the possibility of discontinuing the pre-engineering program, students and faculty once again rose to its defence. Citing themselves as examples, two graduate students argued that the pre-engineering program was the only option open to many students who wished to pursue an engineering education. Neither of them would have graduated with an engineering degree without pre-engineering, and they argued that Waterloo would lose many potentially good undergraduate students who needed this service program.[49]

A.M. Moon, whose role in recommending the province support Co-operative education had been a turning point in the Department of Education's acceptance of the program, and who had left the government to join Waterloo's Co-ordination Department, argued that pre-engineering gave an opportunity to those who would otherwise not necessarily be admitted to the university and an opportunity to some who wanted to get back to school. Commending the university for the development of the program, Moon felt the elimination of pre-engineering would ultimately be a greater loss to the university than its continued operation would be to its finances.[50]

Once again the university hesitated. Considering arguments in favour of preserving the pre-engineering option, the Engineering Faculty Curriculum Committee recommended that the faculty continue the program for another three years. In October 1963, however, Dean Wright sought the immediate elimination of the program, arguing that the educational need for the university's high school equivalency program no longer existed. As Wright pointed out, "From 1957 to 1959, in the early years of the Engineering course at Waterloo, the pre-engineering enrolment was quite significant, reflecting substantial enrolments from those coming either from industry or from technical courses in secondary schools, and others who would not likely have been able to carry on to university studies in Engineering in the

regular fashion. There is little doubt that the pre-engineering year provided for an important need at the time. Our experience since that time has shown that the flow of students from industry into the pre-engineering year has diminished sharply, and the development recently in the province of a more flexible pattern in the secondary schools, providing paths leading to university entrance to students embarking in technical courses, suggests that the essential need for the pre-engineering year is indeed past."[51] This was a way out and Hagey and Needles accepted his explanation.

The momentum quickly shifted to Wright's point of view. The University of Waterloo and the Faculty of Engineering thus eliminated the program that had provided the university its first students and its academic origin. A secondary effect was that students in Co-operative education were now those who maintained a high academic record. This built the reputation of Co-operative education at Waterloo as a flagship program and facilitated its expansion into the Faculties of Arts, Science, Mathematics, and ultimately to Environmental Studies and Applied Health Sciences as well as in Architecture, Accounting, and Pharmacy. Industry and government equated Co-op at Waterloo with academic excellence and students saw it as a prestigious program. This formed a marked contrast to Co-operative programs at other universities, which aimed at attracting primarily disadvantaged students or were limited to specific geographical areas in recruiting both students and participating companies.

"Waterloo's students came from across the province and across Canada. This, too, was novel for such a new university."

As its tenth anniversary neared, the University of Waterloo and its Co-operative program had established a reputation for innovation and excellence. Happily, they joined in celebrating the centenary of Confederation and the tenth anniversary of the University of Waterloo on July 1, 1967. Ira Needles was right. It had been a remarkable decade.

CHAPTER FOUR

Waterloo on the national stage

The traditional dominance of the older Ontario universities influenced Waterloo to chart its own course as a university. As one prominent professor of Engineering explained, "Due to our physical proximity, we are operating in the shadow of the University of Toronto. There is a tendency, among the general public and educational authorities alike, to regard the University of Toronto as the parent university and all other universities, particularly in Ontario, as its subservient satellites. … Our opinion is that we should take immediate initiatives to break the Toronto spell…; otherwise we shall be forever playing second fiddle to Toronto."[1] Waterloo's identity was also driven by the development of the Co-operative education program, which distinguished it from other universities in Canada and which gave it a dominant presence overnight, while the ebullience and self-assuredness of Douglas Wright, whose leadership of Engineering, combined with industry's embrace of Waterloo's students, made his Faculty the University's centrepiece. Engineering also had another advantage: as a profession, it appealed to many who were the first generation of their families to attend university, and this pent-up demand resulted in courses that often were oversubscribed.

becoming outdated, replacing them with more emphasis on truly fundamental and more general theoretical treatments, the academic scene was very much in flux. Returning from the meetings of the Engineering Institute of Canada's educational conference in June 1959, Douglas Wright outlined a blueprint for Engineering at Waterloo.[3] He believed that most Canadian universities had changed very little in their customs, curriculum, and conduct since the mid-1940s. Institutional inertia and a reluctance to make significant structural adjustments intensified the stress in older universities. At most of these universities, he said, senior professors in engineering showed considerable reluctance to change and the issue of curriculum reform was neglected.[4] In preparation for the expected wave of new students, even where there was a willingness to make serious program and curricular changes, funding was not available.[5]

There is a certain irony that Waterloo's initial advantage may have been the absence of a curricular tradition. Without an entrenched program, the Faculty of Engineering was able to introduce its own curriculum and to incorporate within it the implementation of Co-operative education.[6] Wright considered it important to reduce the number of contact hours between students and professors, allowing students more time for individual study and removing tasks which, while relevant to engineering training, were not of university calibre. He eliminated traditional drawing courses and the lab experimentation that had become less important in professional engineering. Whatever experience students required in these elements, Wright foresaw, could be acquired during Co-op work

There was more to it than that. Changes in engineering practice required new methods of training engineering students, for engineering had spilled over more and more into what used to be the exclusive domain of the pure scientist—the physicist and the mathematician. In the opinion of those who were creating Waterloo's engineering curriculum, engineering training needed to be as broad and scientific as possible.[2] Although some engineering departments at other universities had begun to amend their programs to eliminate courses which were terms, allowing more time for an academic curriculum that included mathematics, computer science, and analytical training.

Scientific discoveries earlier in the century had provided a theoretical foundation that needed to be incorporated. Thus, the stress was for a complex, theoretical, scientific and mathematical approach to engineering problems rather than regarding them as merely physical problems to be solved by observation and measurement. In Electrical Engineering, Basil Myers had published papers concerning the theory of graphs and shared a commitment to a strong, theoretical mathematical foundation in engineering. Mathematics became a strong component of Waterloo's program where Ralph Stanton's area of mathematical research, numerical analysis, anticipated computer-assisted solutions to solve mathematical and physical problems.

In February 1961, Wright enthused in a note to Stanton that the ideas at Waterloo were part of a larger debate with international connotations: "I note with some interest," he said, "that at the recent Pan-American Congress on Engineering Education held in Buenos Aires in September of 1960 attended by engineering educators from all of North and South America, a number of resolutions were passed of which Number 6 comments on the particular need for work in Applied Mathematics for engineers, of a sort not previously made available, with the firm recommendations that every university have a laboratory of Applied Mathematics and that every school of engineering have organized courses on Numerical Calculus."[7]

Waterloo's experiment with the Co-operative program also provided an opportunity to segregate some of the traditional skills and to implement a more rigorous academic program. T.L. Batke, Professor of Chemical Engineering and the University's newly-appointed Vice-President, Academic, explained that, "Industry becomes an off-campus faculty which undertakes to teach, perhaps in a more indirect and subtle way the 'art of engineering.'"[8] The Waterloo system, he said, "allowed industry to teach the 'know-how' in engineering, while the academic program would teach the 'know-why.'"[9] In June 1962 Douglas Wright gave a major address to the Annual General Meeting of the Engineering Institute of Canada,[10] and in it he outlined the growth of Engineering at Waterloo and reflected on the ways in which Waterloo's curriculum met the challenges presented in contemporary university education:

It has...been an important five years, [since 1957] when important changes in undergraduate engineering curricula were taking place in many other universities in North America. And beyond this, at Waterloo, there is still freedom from much of the inertia that ordinarily tends to inhibit changes in older universities...

Considerable efforts have been made to remove unessential studies from the core programs, and the best measure of need that has been used in evaluating the appropriateness of various topics is to determine whether they are essential prerequisites for some later study in the course. ...As more analytical techniques (particularly numerical mathematical analysis) have been developed, it has become possible to approach problems of practical engineering complexity with a rigour that was unknown a generation ago... [But Wright also cautioned]...

Although the importance of rigour and analytical ability cannot be under-emphasized, it must be remembered that the essence of engineering is synthesis rather than analysis. The engineer cannot be satisfied with analysing and understanding, but must do and create.[11]

Wright also spoke of the 'new' concept of engineering design being introduced at Waterloo and of the influence in its development of the Hochschule für Gestaltung at Ulm/Donay in West Germany, and he concluded by talking about the importance of the Co-operative plan of education:

It is perhaps also fair to say that the development of the co-operative engineering program at Waterloo is a significant sign of the times. Such a radical step could hardly have been contemplated in Canada before 1950. It is clear that the changing character of the engineering profession demands today a more radical view of objectives and methods than has been required in previous times. There is indication also that the universities in general are preparing to take a more radical view of their position in society. Certainly, we have come to a point in the development of higher education in Canada where heterogeneity in pattern and form is more valuable than dreary uniformity.[12]

Reacting to concerns about the applied nature of Co-operative education at technical or "trade schools," Waterloo demanded a high standard of engineering research, and because of the lack of a strong research tradition in other engineering schools in Canada, a wide opening existed for Waterloo to establish its reputation.[13]

The elimination from its curriculum of an Engineering Physics option separated Waterloo from many other Canadian universities and especially the University of Toronto. Ron Bowman's original appointment to Waterloo in 1957 had been to initiate precisely this program, but when Douglas Wright took over as Dean of Engineering, he immediately sought to eliminate it.[14] Wright disliked the notion of "Engineering Physics as an honours course, with the implication that the rest of engineering was at the pass level," and he regarded it as "intolerable in a professional faculty such as engineering." Instead, he wanted it understood that at Waterloo, "all undergraduate degree courses in engineering are at honours level. ... Certainly, our intention ... is that all our engineering courses should be honour standard." In keeping with the change in direction of Waterloo's curriculum, Wright indicated that "A strong central curriculum – concentrating on science and mathematics – would eliminate the need for Engineering Physics, and all departments would offer courses in modern physics for engineers with particular attention to those branches of modern physics ... which have strong engineering connotations."[15] It took another three years, but in the end Wright's point of view carried the day.[16] It may have taken longer than he intended, but the implications of this change spread to the Faculties of Arts and Science where honours level expectations were imbedded across the university.

For all of its success, by 1962 Dean Wright had written to President Hagey that the members of the Engineering Faculty were suffering from a crisis of morale because they felt that their place in the university was slipping. The focus on the development of Arts, Wright complained, was sacrificing Engineering for a "run of the mill" arts faculty.[17] Having barely recovered from the schism with Waterloo College and rejection by the Evangelical Lutheran Synod, as well as the overt challenge to his presidency by the President of the University of Western Ontario and the reluctance of other university presidents to accept Waterloo as a university of equal stature,[18] Hagey now faced a truculent engineering faculty. When would it all end?

Ironically, as Wright explained to Hagey, "[T]he most important component in the present low morale is a sense of frustration which can be held to be largely due to the successes we have already achieved! ... With some beginning indications that we have indeed been successful here in Engineering, with considerable increases in the numbers of applications for graduate study, it might be thought that there would be widespread elation, and a doubling of efforts for further growth and expansion. Instead, the university's efforts to pursue the developments in Arts committed in 1960 coupled with general pressures on finances have caused a restriction on Engineering at this most critical time. When the number of new appointments in the various faculties are compared, and when it is acknowledged that engineering is probably a dozen appointments short, it is little wonder that people are frustrated."[19]

The Faculty of Engineering also wanted decisions about graduate studies taken from the Dean of Graduate Studies, believing that the Engineering Faculty Council should concern itself with the complete range of engineering education in the university, arguing that the "Engineering Faculty Council as a whole should assume the functions of deciding upon and directing its activities in the field of graduate instruction and the supervision of research. ... There was nothing the Graduate Faculty presently did affecting Engineering which could not more properly and more effectively done within the Engineering Faculty Council."[20] Turf battles were nothing new, as Engineering staked its claim to be the dominant faculty in the university and the emphasis on graduate research became a hallmark of the Waterloo program.

For all of that, all was not entirely well within Engineering's own program. The high failure rate of students enrolled in the engineering curriculum was especially worrisome. At the end of the 1962 term, more than 30% of the first year students had failed, causing the Examinations and Promotions Committee to recommend that the final examination grades be curved to increase the number of passing students.[21] This imperfect solution did not wholly resolve the problem, and the failure rate fluctuated between 27% and 43% in 1963-1964.

When the issue of the high failure rate emerged again, the Faculty of Engineering was at a loss as to how to deal with it. In the face of its rapid development, Engineering lacked a coherent program.[22] A revised undergraduate curriculum, which included general engineering courses and a common first year, was suggested as a solution to end the inordinately large number of student failures.

Ted Batke, the Engineering professor who had been appointed as the University's first Vice-President, Acacemic and always one to muse philosophically, recognized the problems facing a university where rapid growth had not followed a clearly delineated plan. Not all departments were of the same size, nor were they equal in stature – how could they be? He was not even certain that they should be. The uneven development was characteristic of Waterloo's growth, and Batke conceded that it seemed necessary to allow what he described as an "almost explosive development" where the conditions were right and people were available.[23] He also conceded that it would be important to continue to support areas of strength within the university if Waterloo was to become a fine university, as distinct from merely a large university and he was determined to pursue academic excellence, quality, and character in the general life of the university community.

Like everyone who thought about Waterloo in those days, Batke identified that Waterloo's chief strength had been its flexibility and willingness to explore new directions. This, he said, "has made it difficult to establish a detailed master plan for the future and is a price we pay for being unconventional." He also conceded that "the university's image has been, and still is, based largely on Co-operative education. Since we are unique in this respect and have assumed the role of leadership, it is essential to our total well-being that Co-operative education be of high calibre and well done." Batke's report in June 1964 to the Board of Governors highlighted the successes of the university and called for a time to take stock and to plan for the future.[24]

The hurly-burly of a new university had been overwhelming. Until this point, everyone had been scrambling, detouring around the construction of new buildings to avoid the inevitable mud and debris, with faculty and students often crowded together in still-uncompleted classrooms. Books were needed for the library and equipment for the laboratories. The Batke report, however, signalled that a moment had come to take a second breath as the 1963/64 academic year marked a transition in the university's life.

The Faculty of Arts, created in the wake of the emotional split with Waterloo College, had emerged as a significant part of the University of Waterloo. Taken together, the enrolment of the faculties of Arts and Science now equalled Engineering's and soon would surpass it. For the first time in 1963 each of the undergraduate departments across the university had a full undergraduate program. Graduate work was underway in fourteen of the university's twenty-one departments and faculty research grants totalling half a million dollars had been awarded by outside agencies. The first National Research Council's post-doctoral fellow had arrived on campus. The University of Waterloo was coming of age.

As Batke explained, "the university has, with remarkable success, passed through Phase I, – that of becoming founded – [and] must now consider the directions which will enable it to become a distinguished centre of learning." And he predicted, "The next six years or so, Phase II, will be of crucial importance and the criteria of success will differ somewhat from those of Phase I."[25] The growth of internal structures and the increase in quality during this period will be of far greater importance, he suggested, than the growth in numbers, and the chief element and guiding criterion of the years immediately ahead must be high academic quality in research, scholarship and teaching, as well as in the general intellectual and social life of the whole university community. It was clearly time to take stock and to reflect on the idea of the university and its direction for the future; easier said than done for a university that had so little time for introspection.

President Hagey once again found himself in the midst of a debate that threatened the university idea that he had championed. In the past, in academic decisions, Hagey had deferred to his deans, and especially to Douglas Wright. Hagey's own background, like that of his mentor, Ira Needles, had been in Arts and his vision for Waterloo went beyond its Faculty of Engineering. Still, the sense of importance felt by the engineering faculty was understandable.[26] Engineering at Waterloo had

a freshman enrolment of over 550 students – the largest in Canada – and with more than 400 Canadian corporations and organizations in six provinces actively cooperating with it in the training of its students, how could it not feel important? In these days of heady optimism, the Dean of Engineering, Douglas Wright, announced that Waterloo's plan was to grow to a steady state of undergraduate enrolment of over 2000, larger than any engineering school in Canada and "of the order of size of most of the principal engineering schools in the United States."[27] Wright repeated a refrain that he had often used in his public remarks emphasizing the University of Waterloo's sense of its unique place among Canadian universities: "In undertaking a radical approach to engineering education in Canada it seemed to us that anything short of conspicuous success would indeed be failure. With the freedom for experimentation that was available in a young university, it became equally clear that a goal of excellence was appropriate and necessary. The resulting determination to excel has clearly been one of our most significant features and assets in these seven years of development... I hope and trust that our determination to excel will not diminish."[28] Rhetorically powerful, Wright's comments also evoke the determination of the University of Waterloo to establish its identity and its reputation.

WATERLOO ON THE NATIONAL STAGE: EXPO 67

Waterloo's reputation gained further prominence when its Institute of Design succeeded in winning three contracts for the international world's fair, Expo 67.[29] As Canadians gathered together with newfound pride to celebrate the centennial of their nation, the eyes of the world turned to Montréal and to the marvels of its international World's Fair. Waterloo's Institute of Design, first mooted in 1962 and created formally in 1964, moved onto the national stage with a contract from the Canadian Corporation for the 1967 World Exhibition for the design of two theme buildings, the Kaleidoscope Pavilion and the Man and his Planet and Space Pavilion. Professor George Soulis, who initiated the Institute at the suggestion of Dean Wright, explained that the creation of an Institute of Design ".... [gave] to Canada a unique facility which would eminently serve Canadian society and enhance the reputation of the University of Waterloo."[30] The Waterloo-designed Kaleidoscope Pavilion at Expo 67 turned out to be one of the most popular exhibits in the World's Fair and was exceeded in numbers of visitors only by three national pavilions, those of Canada, the United States, and the Soviet Union. The Man and his Planet and Space Pavilion was also extremely popular and symbolic of the future face of Waterloo's research, while a third successful exhibit in industrial design sponsored by the Bata Shoe company was developed by graduate students from Waterloo. International recognition for a university that celebrated its 10th anniversary on the day that Canada marked its 100th birthday instilled a sense of pride that was shared in Waterloo and Ottawa.

FUTURE THINK? THE DEBATE INTENSIFIES

Despite this conspicuous success, Engineering's view of the world was not universally shared. The belief that since Waterloo's "historical strength" had been in engineering, Waterloo should be an engineering school was challenged by members of other faculty councils who suggested that perhaps there were other ways to measure success in university education. This was not an altogether new debate, and in the past the Deans of Arts and Science had been sensitive to Engineering's perception of its diminished share of scarce resources as well as its occasional arrogance and attitude of superiority. Partly in response to this perception, members of the Arts and Science Faculties noted that it is in the nature of things for universities to develop certain ratios of arts, science, and engineering, and when compared to the usual ratio between arts and engineering at all other universities it was only a function of Waterloo's hurried growth that the arts faculty was relatively small.[31] The arrival on the campus of senior scholars such as Noel Hynes in Biology, K.A. MacKirdy in History, George Hibbard in English, J.W. Leach in Physics, and Paul Seligman in Philosophy gave added stature to what had once been faculties struggling to achieve prominence. E.L. (Ernie) Holmes, filling in for Dean Wright on the University Planning Committee, was clearly agitated by the notion that the other faculties had an important role to play in the university's future. As he reported to the Engineering Council, "This sort of comment would indicate that as a university we have no concern for influencing our own destiny but rather we are allowing a natural pattern to emerge. The question we must ask ourselves is whether or not this is the type of university we wish to have at Waterloo.

Is it in the interests of ourselves, the province, and perhaps the future of the country for us to develop as a traditional university, or should we consider the possibility of developing in some special way, such as having a planned emphasis on engineering, mathematics, science, and the social sciences?"[32] The gauntlet had been thrown down.

Holmes raised the rhetorical debate to a new level in September 1966 when he complained to the planning committee that by supporting the growth of arts and other new programs, the university was spreading its resources too thinly. With unaccustomed belligerence, he suggested that in light of the Faculty of Arts lowering its admission average to meet its enrolment projections, "Could not the space in arts have been used for the bookstore, etc. so that engineering need not turn away well-qualified applicants?"[33] He did not mention, of course, that the university bookstore was located in Engineering II or that in its formative years Engineering's own admission standards were sometimes dubious. Nonetheless, rising to the bait, the Engineering Faculty Council challenged the President's commission on university planning and development to clearly decide on the place that the University of Waterloo hoped to take in the "provincial, national and international scenes." This document merits consideration as the expression of Engineering's official point of view and of the idea of "national" or even "international importance" associated with the then-current notion of the place of engineering in Canadian society:

The Engineering Planning Committee contends that unless this university makes the decision to build on its present areas of strength, it will never become a great university, but must be content to be a run-of-the-mill Ontario School. It is suggested that this decision must be reached quickly and furthermore an official announcement of our intentions should be released to the public. Any delay may mean that we could be politically out-manoeuvred by another institution which is, in at least one of our particular areas of strength, currently less well equipped particularly in terms of the potential within its faculty...The goal of the Faculty of Engineering of the University of Waterloo is to become internationally recognized as among the world's leading schools of engineering. It must become firmly established as the elite engineering school in Canada – or at least "one of three." At the present time, there is no great engineering school in Canada. The achievements of the past few years clearly indicate

that the faculty of engineering of the University of Waterloo has now the greatest potential of any engineering school in Canada and accordingly asks full support of the President's Council in order that it may realize this potential and become a great school of engineering...

It is likely that in pursuing the suggested policy of building on strength the University might need to concentrate its resources and not spread itself thinly by further expansion in the more traditional Arts honours or general programs in English, Latin, French etc. subject areas which are, incidentally, very well covered at a high level in other universities in the province...

If this University takes a positive attitude and clearly states its aims, it may well establish itself in an advantageous position in terms of obtaining special earmarked funds to enable it to achieve excellence in areas of concern connected with the future economic development of the province and the nation. If this university does not take this stand, another university will undoubtedly act and, at least as far as engineering is concerned, it is suggested that this would not be in the best economic interests of either Ontario or Canada—or the University of Waterloo.[34]

President Hagey was not so certain. His goal was to create a multi-faculty university and he hesitated to identify the university's future too narrowly. Nor was he convinced that the province was prepared to support the initiative proposed by Engineering. In reply to the criticism that engineering's growth could be adversely affected by support for the Faculty of Arts, he emphasized that the strength of the University of Waterloo was its willingness to accept new programs and that the development of new programs in other faculties did not necessarily affect or hold back the Faculty of Engineering. As an effort at conciliation, however, Hagey indicated his pleasure in the goal of the Engineering faculty to become a national and international centre of excellence and he encouraged the Faculty to document its case in a brief on the subject. The debate was far from over.

Chemical engineering professor Donald Scott was only too happy to comply and he challenged President Hagey's reading of provincial priorities. Scott was not alone in his sense of the opportunity for Waterloo to re-write the history of engineering education in Canada, but his is the most comprehensive statement sent to the president.[35] As he explained in a letter to Dr. Hagey on October 17, 1966:

One might assume that much of the academic nature of this University will be dictated by the Province. Such an assumption need not be true. The Province might well prevent us from embarking on too costly or speculative a program, but if this University proposed to build upon and expand in areas of demonstrated competence, such an avowed purpose would surely meet with both the approval and support of the Province.

In Canada, there is not now, and never has been, a university sufficiently devoted to the Applied Sciences (in the broad sense) to be willing to channel its resources into the pursuit of excellence in these fields. There has never been a Canadian institution which even pretended to make an attempt to be a counterpart of such successful technical universities as the Massachusetts Institute of Technology or the Imperial College of Science and Technology....

If we elect to build intensively on our present areas of strength, which surely is in the applied sciences, specifically applied Mathematics, social sciences and engineering, then something uniquely excellent, and uniquely able to contribute to provincial and national welfare can be evolved. This evolution would not by any means preclude expansion, but expansion must then be in related or complementary areas of applied science and technology, such as applied chemistry, physics and biology, or be in further development in social sciences, engineering and mathematics. I do not propose to argue the purist's concept of a university, except to note that a technological society does indeed have need of the humanities, fine arts, and pure science, but scholarly work in these areas is done much better elsewhere that it is now being done here, or can be expected to be done for some considerable time.

Academic excellence can only be achieved by concerted and single-minded effort, and by liberal financial resources. For an institution of the present and probable future size and resources of this university, it means that excellence will only be achieved by deliberately pursuing it in a limited number of areas, and this means academic specialization. On the basis of our present strengths and the provincial and national need, the applied sciences are the only logical area for this pursuit of excellence. In fact, the need is so great at this time in the nation's history, that if this University does not pursue this course, others will, and our initial strengths will decline to a place of lesser national significance in the university picture. It

is interesting to note that of all the industrialized nations of the world, Canada is the only one which has not produced a major technical university of good reputation.

President Hagey, however, had his own dreams for the future development of the University of Waterloo and they were cast on a larger scale than Donald Scott's prescription. Hagey foresaw the recently-acquired 800 acre North Campus as providing the possibility of Waterloo being a major, full scale international university. He predicted having there a medical school and a law school as well as two "colleges" similar in size to the South Campus with an enrolment in Arts and Science that placed Waterloo among the best North American universities, and he foresaw a new administration building along the Columbia Street entrance to the campus that would offset the hurried entrance to the campus that had been rushed into being in 1958. Hagey's determination to see Waterloo as a full comprehensive school and not as a technological university was further demonstrated when he approved construction of the Humanities Building, with facilities to house the Departments of History, English and Philosophy along with a 721 seat "Humanities Theatre" suitable for dramatic productions. His point was well made.

Scott's arguments were not without interest and earlier might have met with greater success. Time had moved on and so had the province's willingness to pursue such a specialized initiative. As one indication of this, a new granting formula for the funding of universities based on enrolment, rather than special projects, was initiated. This was regarded as a landmark achievement that, for the first time, introduced a system of equality between newer and older universities, eliminating the advantaged position of more established universities. It also meant that the special status sought by Donald Scott was unlikely. The author of the funding formula was none other than Douglas Wright, Waterloo's former Dean of Engineering, who left the University in 1966 and became the first Chair of Ontario's Committee on University Affairs in 1967.[36] The growth of so many new universities (Trent, Windsor, Brock, Guelph, Laurentian, Lakehead, and York) led the province to reconsider its funding priorities, and Wright's system of formula-derived grants was the first step. Next, Wright chaired a special commission to broadly study the entire system of

postsecondary education in Ontario and to make recommendations for its rationalization. There was no turning back the clock.

A NEW ERA FOR ONTARIO'S UNIVERSITIES

The euphoria surrounding the success of Expo 67, which had coincided with the most remarkable decade in Waterloo's history, came to an abrupt end the next year when a national economic slowdown resulted in severe constraints and limited resources for Ontario's universities. Between the end of Canada's centennial celebrations in 1967 and the pressures to make engineering more socially relevant came 1968, "the year that shook the world."[37] It threatened the relevance of universities and challenged democratic and social values worldwide. Lost in the rhetoric for change was Donald Scott's outline of Waterloo's future. The unwavering acceptance of engineering was called into question as the success of technology in the conduct of World War II was replaced by the technological excess of the Cold War, followed by daily televised broadcasts of the failure of technology to win the war in Vietnam. Two books describing this era illustrate the contrast: Pierre Berton's *1967 The Last Good Year* (Toronto, 1997) revels in the excitement and success of Canada's centennial celebrations and Mark Kurlansky's *1968: The Year That Rocked The World* (New York, 2004) outlines the trauma that engulfed international communities as techno-values were rejected and replaced with a profound desire for more humanistic ideas, and a yearning for new values to emerge.

Dramatic changes in students' clothes, music, and lifestyles were an outward sign that times had changed. The now quaint and old-fashioned protest music of the earlier sixties and the rock-a-billy sounds of Bo Didley and Rompin' Ronnie Hawkins, which had been a mainstay of the Waterloo campus and student dances, was replaced by the Beatles' new concept album, *Sgt. Pepper's Lonely Hearts Club Band*, transporting rock into the psychedelic future and marking a new era, along with the sounds of the Grateful Dead, Jefferson Airplane, and Big Brother and the Holding Company with Janis Joplin. The moderate, non-confrontational style of student leaders was displaced by the effusive, energetic political style that coalesced into the "political theatre" of the yippees. Students at Waterloo discarded their once-prized Engineering jackets, thin ties, tweed sports coats, and short-cropped hairstyles. Long flowing hair, exuberant mutton chop sideburns, and bushy, scraggy beards became the order of the day. Photographs of these Waterloo students in the university yearbooks bear little resemblance to those who had gone before them.

These were turbulent times for university students across North America. The latter part of the decade was an era of student protest, giving a label to the '60s as one of seemingly unending radicalism. University campuses erupted in student demonstrations, and in the final years of the decade, between October 1967 and May 1969, 471 "riots" and "disorders" occurred at 211 separate universities in the United States, leading to 6,158 arrests and 645 expulsions. In Canada, violence rocked the country when students blockaded the administration offices of Sir George Williams University in Montreal, throwing computer cards out the windows, destroying student records, and damaging parts of the university building.[38]

Without fear of being drafted to fight in a war in Vietnam, which most students thought was both unjust and unwinnable, students at Waterloo were less directly affected by the turmoil that faced so many university students in the United States. The medium of television, however, had brought this war and the protests against it onto every university campus and into every living room. It simply could not be ignored, and it fed the sense of unrest felt by so many students. Authority everywhere was questioned as pressure to excel in university seemed ever to intensify, while the assurance that a job would be waiting immediately after graduation no longer existed.

In the fall of 1967 protests against recruiting on campus by Dow Chemical, which manufactured the napalm being used in Vietnam occurred in the United States where 27 separate demonstrations were directed against Dow Chemical. Protests began in Canada at the University of Toronto when students attempted to block the entrance to the university's recruiting centre by lying in front of its entrance. In the face of this intense protest, University of Toronto officials suspended interviews on campus.[39] This had become a cause celebre among university students. What then of Waterloo? The debate at Waterloo was both more complex and qualitatively different. Here, University security officers gathered to ensure the safety of the Co-op recruiters, including those from Dow Chemical, and engineering students rallied against attempts to restrict the Dow Chemical's representatives from coming on campus and meeting with students. It was the students' right to choose and they would not have this fundamental right limited by "radical protestors." They protested against the protestors. The confrontation dissipated. Radical in some ways, Waterloo was also a very conservative campus. Although students from all of the faculties had participated in a previous "sit-in" at the University bookstore when the issue was the high price of text books and supplies and the profit made by the University from books that students were required to purchase. As students sang freedom songs, played cards, and badgered those who tried to make a purchase, the book store staff continued to conduct business as usual. When the students marched to President Hagey's office to have their demands heard, he agreed to act on their concerns. Then it was over. Bookstore prices were lowered and life returned to normal – or did it?

The Students' Council, which had come under the sway of the "Radical Students' Movement," sought to become involved in the larger off-campus social and political issues, by passing a resolution that the University of Waterloo officially support Americans who were resisting their country's war effort by refusing to serve in its armed forces. So radical a motion was strongly opposed by the Engineering Society which immediately circulated a petition calling for a student referendum. Many students voted, with 1676 of them rejecting council support for the "draft dodgers." The editors of *The Chevron*, the newly re-named and now radical student newspaper, announced the defeat with the headline: "No longer the Red University." In the era of student unrest, this campus and this University took on a decidedly different look from so many other universities in Canada and across North America. Before the decade was over *The Chevron* was also gone, replaced in 1978 by a new student newspaper, *Imprint*, and a reorganized and more representative students' council.

As the "generation gap" challenged order and older ways of doing things, the administrative leadership at Waterloo changed. In 1967, Howard Petch, the former Principal of Hamilton College at McMaster University, replaced Ted Batke as Vice President, Academic. Almost as soon as he arrived, Petch found himself propelled into new responsibilities when President Hagey unexpectedly left for cancer treatment at Princess Margaret Hospital in Toronto. Petch became his own Vice President as he stood in for an ailing president. This was made official in 1969 when Petch was appointed President Pro-Tem, but in many ways he had been acting as president from the moment he arrived. The Dean of Arts, Norman High, retired in June 1967, to be replaced by J.S. Minas; Douglas Wright retired as Dean of Engineering in June 1966 and was succeeded by A.N. Sherbourne; Ralph Stanton completed his term as Chair of Mathematics and on November 21, 1966 David Sprott became the first Dean of the newly-formed Faculty of Mathematics. In Science, W.A.E. McBryde, whose administrative career began as Acting Dean of Science in December 1960 and as Dean in January 1961, stepped down in 1969. A new president arrived in July 1970 when Burton Matthews, at the age of forty-four, became Waterloo's second president. Immediately, he faced a group of truculent deans eager to assert their authority and to test his mettle; he was also confronted by raucous student leaders proclaiming themselves to be part of a Radical Student's Movement, a Faculty Association seeking to find its place in the university, and the reorganization of the University's governing structure. These were challenging times for universities, students, faculty members, staff, and administrators alike. Matthews succeeded admirably. A hands-on president, he reorganized Dean's Council, quieted student unrest, dealt with the insecurity created by the FLQ crisis in October 1970, which sent shivers across university campuses and sent undercover RCMP officers to Waterloo,[40] and brought about an era of trust and goodwill in the university's relationship with the faculty and staff associations in the long-lasting Matthews-Dubinski agreement.[41] He did all this while keeping intact the restless spirit of innovation that had marked the Waterloo experiment in its first decade.

In 1968 the provincial government informed the University that it was not prepared to approve a building extension to the university's engineering complex. By 1972 there was an arbitrary freeze on capital construction at all Ontario universities. The philosophy of growth in Ontario's universities was replaced by one of careful cost accounting. At the same time, the provincial mood about universities shifted from optimism to cautious restraint and one Ontario study, headed by David Dodge, a future Governor of the Bank of Canada, concluded that the economic return on investment in professions such as engineering was actually negative.[42] The problem at Waterloo and elsewhere in the province was no longer how to encourage growth, but how best to sustain what was built. A.N. Sherbourne, a former classmate of Wright's at Cambridge University who replaced Wright as Dean of Engineering in 1966, shared many of Wright's preconceptions about the central importance of engineering. However, he also faced new and different times as the Ontario government introduced new funding formulas and sought to impose specific ideas about university education, limits on expansion, and an embargo on new programs.

Sherbourne's leadership provided an opportunity to build a quality of excellence in engineering teaching and research as he recruited senior research scholars from around the world to join Engineering at Waterloo. A report commissioned by the University's Engineering Faculty, however, also noted a changed environment. "No longer," the authors proclaimed, "is there the gung-ho feeling of dynamism and experimentation."[43] Perhaps they were right. Faculty members were more settled, research projects became more structured, and engineering debates became more managed and less frequent, while the faculty itself was larger in number and more complex. But others, like Engineering Professor Savvas Chamberlain, remember this as a time when research was exciting and the Faculty was strongly committed to developing research programs. He recalls a cohort of active researchers often working together on new initiatives.[44] Perhaps it was also true that the more things changed, the more they remained the same. This would not be the first time that this adage was applicable to life at Waterloo.

THE LAPP REPORT: ENGINEERING UNDER FIRE

In the midst of this turbulence, in the province's first effort at academic planning for the Ontario university system, Dr. Philip Lapp was commissioned to undertake a comprehensive review of engineering

education in the province. In his 1971 report on engineering in Ontario,[45] dubbed the "ring of iron," with observations and recommendations regarding the quality of Ontario's engineering education, Lapp concluded that all was not well! As part of the remedy for this malady, Lapp recommended that Waterloo's Faculty of Engineering become a separate technical university with its own board of governors. Burton Matthews, the university's new president, was strongly opposed. He rejected the sundering of engineering from the university and felt that separate status would be less efficient than engineering's position within the university. But what of the Faculty of Engineering? What was their response? Was it not what some of them had indirectly been advocating? Dean Sherbourne was loath to become involved in the debate. Instead, a "study committee" was created which criticized the recommendation that engineering become a technical university. Lapp's recommendation, the committee concluded, "rested on little substance and superficial considerations" and the committee suggested the report, known as the "Ring of iron" be "allowed to rust."[46]

CHANGING TIMES:
NEW CHALLENGES FOR WATERLOO

As the baby boom generation entered the school system, and as elementary and high schools expanded, the demand for arts and science graduates grew exponentially, as did enrolment in these two faculties. In the face of these changing times, Waterloo responded by expanding its Arts and Science faculties and by creating new interdisciplinary programs such as Canadian Studies and Women's Studies. New faculties such as Environmental Studies, Human Kinetics and Leisure Studies (which ultimately became Applied Health Sciences) reinforced the University's spirit of innovation. The development of new faculties and programs was an indication of the societal relevance of Waterloo's mission as a university free to establish

its own traditions. In Science, Professors James Leslie and Ted Dixon introduced the concept of distance education through taped lectures for a broadening market and a wider delivery of university education, and their initiative was adopted across the university. As the Faculty of Engineering revised its focus, the societal changes that had given Co-operative education and Waterloo's Engineering program pre-eminence in the 1960s began to pull the university in new directions.

Canada's need for 150,000 engineers proclaimed by Ira Needles in 1956 was no longer the rallying cry for this generation of students. The expansion of other universities and shifting social priorities had resulted in a surfeit of engineers. The Lapp Report noted that in 1969/1970 only two Ontario universities, Waterloo and Toronto, had enrolments above the minimum required for efficient programming. Three others had enrolments near the minimum, and enrolment in each of the other six engineering programs at Ontario's universities was "well below the minimum." Simply put, the report concluded, "Ontario has more engineering programs than can be justified by any criteria other than the need for geographical distribution."[47]

The economic downturn of the 1970s, decreasing numbers of undergraduate students choosing engineering, and a provincial embargo on new graduate programs which had been announced in 1971 provided the opportunity for the Faculty of Engineering at Waterloo to reaffirm its relationship with industry and, in the atmosphere of uncertainty and change, to encourage faculty members to initiate new collaborative research initiatives. Building on its existing applied research culture, the Engineering Faculty seized the opportunity to play a relevant role in the community. New research in areas such as environmental regulation, medical engineering, and bioengineering as well as in resource and transportation planning, energy and society emerged as areas of Waterloo's strength.[48]

INTELLECTUAL PROPERTY: THE WATERLOO PRECEDENT

Waterloo was the first university in Canada to respond to the federal government's proposal to establish an Industrial Research Institute to facilitate cooperation between the faculty, industry, and government.[49] As part of the protocol established by the government, Waterloo had to appoint the chair of the Institute from Canadian industry. Dean Sherbourne and Ernie Holmes persuaded Jim Tomecho to leave Canadian Industries in Montreal to come to Waterloo. Before his career in industry, Tomecho had played professional football with the Saskatchewan Rough Riders and at age 60 still had the build of someone who dominated every room he entered, and like Ira Needles, his physical presence was imposing. Active in the work of Frontier College, which brought literacy to unskilled workers in remote areas of Canada, he shared much of Needles' and Hagey's enthusiasm for the importance of education. He was also well regarded in the Canadian business community. Of all of the contributions arising from the initiatives of the Industrial Research Institute, none would be more important than the creation of Waterloo's unique attitude toward professors' ownership of the intellectual property that they created while employed by the University. As a university without established policies in many areas, Waterloo needed a patent policy to deal with discoveries that emerged from the Industrial Research Institute. Ernie Holmes, the Administrator for the Faculty of Engineering and its member on the patent committee, strongly believed that patents should be held by the inventor, not by the university. At first, Tomecho was not in favour of this idea. It was opposite to the practice in industry, and not done this way at other universities. Holmes persisted and Tomecho relented.[50] Holmes's proposal then went to the Industrial Research Institute's Advisory council, the members of which, as Holmes recalled, were appointees and friends of Jim Tomecho. At first they, too, were opposed. They

were businessmen, and in business and industry ideas or inventions remained the property of the company. But, as Holmes suggested, Tomecho had spoken to them privately and after expressing their contrary point of view, they supported the recommendation about individual ownership.

It was not really a hard sell since most of the members were also serving on the Industrial Advisory Council, which was created to assist in the development of the Co-operative program, and they knew the university and its reputation for thinking outside of the box. What emerged was a patent policy that allowed for the professors' ownership of individual patents, and this immediately became the practice in all aspects of ownership of intellectual property. In 1984 when Holmes became Dean of Research this was the modus vivendi that was followed across the university and was responsible for encouraging many researchers to develop their ideas in commercial markets. So successful was this that under the administration of President Douglas Wright, a minor furor was created by a business magazine which referred to the University as "Waterloo Limited," with the implicit suggestion that applied research and spin-off companies based on university research had displaced the importance of pure research. Nothing could have been further from the truth, but it was also true that Waterloo encouraged and supported the application of research for the betterment of the community.[51]

The social and political unrest in the early 1970s had also caused the Faculty of Engineering to take a more careful measure of its place within the University and within Canadian society, and it emerged more clearly focused with a new and relevant purpose. Waterloo expanded its engineering programs to international commitments with CUSO [Canadian University Students Overseas] in Cuba and with CIDA [the Canadian International Development Agency] in Africa and South

America, including the establishment of an engineering school in Nigeria at the University of Ibadam. These initiatives were strongly supported by Dean Sherbourne and President Matthews, and in 1973 a formal exchange program was established with the University of Paraiba in Brazil.[52] These were precedents for the later creation of Engineers Without Borders by Waterloo engineering graduates George Roter and Parker Mitchell in 2000. Originally student-inspired, other professional engineering chapters of Engineers Without Borders soon followed.

When W. A. McLaughlin succeeded A.N. Sherbourne as Dean of the largest engineering faculty in Canada, he announced that engineering education "should teach students to be aware of environmental issues" and to use their knowledge "to benefit humanity" rather than seeking "short-term economic developments."[53] This came, in part, from McLaughlin's background growing up in Saskatchewan, and it was also a sign of his pragmatic understanding of universities, as under his leadership, engineering at Waterloo settled into a new role focusing on the university's development. In this he was aided by the appointment of former engineering professor T.A. Brzustowski who replaced Howard Petch as the university's Vice President, Academic when Petch left Waterloo to become President of the University of Victoria.

Having survived the worst of the student unrest of the late 60s and early 70s, a number of engineering professors created the Sandford Fleming Foundation and Scholarship program to fund scholarships through donations from faculty, students, professional engineers, and engineering companies. The response from students was heartening, as the admission average of Waterloo's engineering students increased to 81% with nearly half of the students having averages in excess of 90%. Not only did more and better students choose to enter Engineering at Waterloo, but in the face of a second wave of the women's movement and increases in women's participation in the job market, Dean McLaughlin successfully moved toward increasing the number of women students in engineering. By the spring of 1980, Engineering had more than 200 women registered "in a sea of 3000 men."[54] The forces shaping engineering education were felt across Canada, and Waterloo was no exception. Increased female participation in university studies more than offset the decline created by the disappearance of the "baby boomers." Although total university enrolment in the late 1970s grew by a modest 23.6%, increased participation of women constituted 86% of this growth. The impact was also felt in Waterloo's Co-operative education programs where the ever-increasing number of female students challenged the existing job placements and where new coordinators were brought into the program. Long in the past was Lloyd Jones's assurance that he knew personally the employers who would hire Waterloo's students. Long in the past, too, was the requirement that every coordinator be a professional engineer or that they should all be men.

Engineering's plan to increase its funding through entrepreneurial activities set the course for the university's dramatic renewal in the next decade. The return of Douglas Wright in 1981 as the university's third president reaffirmed this direction. Although not without some resistance and controversy from the more traditional areas within the university, Wright began to shift Waterloo from what had been predominantly government funding to seeking support through licenses and innovation with industry and government. A new word, "entrepreneurial," entered the Waterloo lexicon, along with the other watchword of the day, "technology transfer." The principle of faculty members' ownership of intellectual property, which had first been introduced in 1972, encouraged and sustained the university's reputation for entrepreneurial initiatives. The establishment of an Industrial Innovation Centre in 1979 whose specific purpose was "to stimulate an increase in the quantity and quality of technological innovation in Canada in the form of new products [and] new processes for new businesses by working in closer cooperation with faculties of

science, engineering and business" could not have been better timed. The university itself created the Waterloo Process Development Centre as a means of channelling this new activity.

Much of this development depended on the entrepreneurial drive of individual professors. Savvas Chamberlain's company, Dalsa Corporation, founded in 1980 – an industry leader in digital imaging and semiconductor technology, employing approximately 1000 people worldwide with sales revenue of more than $168 million – was developed out of research that he had conducted in electrical engineering at Waterloo. Similarly, Northern Digital Inc., with worldwide markets in measurement technology, was spun off from the University of Waterloo through research developed by Jerry Kris in the Computer Systems Group, while CEO of Northern Digital David Crouch, a Waterloo engineering graduate, began his career there as a Waterloo Co-op student. Initiatives such as these confirmed the innovative reputation of Waterloo, setting the path for its future role within Canada and among the leading universities in the nation in the number of spin-off companies transferring ideas from the university laboratories to the marketplace.

In the face of continued restrictions on university funding, including the ability to fund replacement appointments, and grim reports for the future of engineering education, the University of Waterloo faced severe challenges. These were met in a number of creative ways and in part by the university's reputation as one of Canada's foremost engineering schools. In 1982 a Montreal aerospace company, Com Dev International, relocated to the Waterloo region to benefit from the excellence of Waterloo's graduates as well as the proximity to its research facilities.[55] Com Dev's successful launch of its communications satellite into space completed the circle that had begun with the Russian Sputnik in 1957. It also began a remarkable friendship with the University of Waterloo when in 1997, Valentine O'Donovan, Com Dev's founder and CEO, accepted the position of Chancellor of the University. A generous donor to the university and an inspiring chancellor, O'Donovan's urbanity and his leadership assisted in moving Waterloo and its engineering faculty forward in its relationship to the community and within the university itself and led to the relocation of

the University's School of Architecture to its acclaimed campus on the banks of the Grand River in Cambridge.

BILL LENNOX RETURNS

The appointment of William C. Lennox in 1982 to succeed Wallace McLaughlin as Dean of Engineering seemed particularly fitting. Many fondly remembered Bill Lennox as a member of the first class of engineering students in 1957. His classmates recalled his academic standing in the classroom, his ebullient character, and the pranks that students managed in the midst of a gruelling workload which gave engineering at Waterloo immediate recognition and became part of the folklore of the university. In 1958 he played the drum in the Engineering "band" as students installed their university sign at the corner of King and Dearborn saying ENGINEERING, arts and science, with engineering the most prominent. The creation of a University of Waterloo engineering jacket with a pocket for a whisky flask and another for a slide rule is a legacy of these years. What many remember best is the great water tower caper, when three engineering students scaled the city's water tower on Lester Street to paint the word BEER prominently near the top of the tower.[56] The students who had started at Waterloo in October 1957 were frustrated that their university seemed to be virtually unknown. "When we went home," one of the students, Mike Matthews, recalls, "people would ask, [referring to co-op] 'what's this silly thing about you working in a factory every other semester?'" The students wanted to do something to draw attention to their university and in a brave and daring adventure, in the dark of night, three of them climbed the Lester Street water tower, with Matthews hanging over the side in a quickly devised harness, to paint the word beer in large letters in red "rustoleum" metal paint. Having successfully completed their task, they were disappointed the next day when they saw their handiwork and discovered that because of the curve on the face of the water tower the BEER was not as visible as they had hoped. Not to be deterred, the class as a whole decided that there should be a record of the achievement. Since some of the students were trained pilots, they decided to rent an airplane and have the adventurers go to the

top of the tower and stand there, shaking hands, while the airplane flew over to photograph them for posterity. The airplane failed to appear and the students came down to find a crowd of spectators, including many from their engineering class, as well as several police officers. The students were arrested, photographs taken, and as Matthews recalls, the officers were "giggling the whole time." Two of the students were charged with public mischief, which was then reduced to trespassing. When the case was heard the magistrate spoke severely to the two, saying to them, "You could have been injured or you could have fallen into the water and drowned. I'd hate to think of how Waterloo's water supply would have been contaminated then. We'd mourn your loss, but we would also suffer the loss of our water supply." The students were to pay the cost of repainting the beer section of the water tower, and a "water tower fund" established by Vera Leavoy, a university staff member, raised more than enough to pay the cost. In the end, everyone was happy. The local newspaper ran a photo of the beer tower and national notoriety soon followed as the incident caught the imagination of Canadians coast-to-coast.

This was one of many adventures led by Waterloo's engineers. A Mennonite buggy, as much an icon of the region as the love of beer, was placed on the roof of the Waterloo College administration building.[57] At Halloween, a Volkswagen was carefully installed on the front porch of the Waterloo College women's residence. Not to be outdone by the water tower incident, the alternating class of engineering students placed a large banner on the front façade of the Waterloo Hotel proclaiming it as Home of the Engineers. As the banner was hung, the President of the Engineering Society was busy distracting the police officer at the corner of King and Erb streets. The Waterloo Hotel was officially renamed Annex Five and for several weeks the hotel's owners happily allowed the banner to remain in place.

Bill Lennox's term as dean coincided with the return of Douglas Wright as Waterloo's president. Together, Lennox and Wright sought to recapture the excitement and success of the formative first decade, and by and large they succeeded. Waterloo's students shared in the excitement as their professors began new research in applied areas of technology and as the computer age dawned in its full glory with the creation of the Institute for Computer Research, which drew together researchers from Computer Science, Electrical and Computer Engineering, Mechanical Engineering, and research groups from across the campus interested in Information Technology. More than 80 professors and 200 graduate students became associated with the ICR.[58] This synergy culminated in government support for creating the landmark William G. Davis Centre for Computer Research, which combined Waterloo's research in computing, engineering, and information technology. Based on the idea of the Stanford University Forum and providing a unique window into university research, the Institute began to invite companies to campus to build on the interface between university research and corporate applications of what was often considered "pure" research. This initiative renewed the nascent idea of developing a University research park on the North Campus, an idea whose time came only in 2005 when under a new President, David Johnston, a unique blend of some forty million dollars in university, municipal, provincial, and federal funding opportunities made it possible. The infrastructure was in place to build Waterloo's Research and Technology Park, but the idea behind it had a long genesis.

When David Burns replaced Bill Lennox as dean in 1990, he brought with him a wealth of experience from Great Britain and a determination to maintain the leadership position of engineering at Waterloo. During his administration, however, the university faced massive cutbacks in funding from the provincial government. Like the rest of the university, Engineering suffered significant losses as the Special Early Retirement Package known by the acronym of SERP, introduced as a way of maintaining the integrity of the university in a time of adversity, came into play. The retirement plan was a bold initiative by President James Downey and Vice-President, Academic and Provost Jim Kalbfleisch, supported by the Faculty and Staff Associations that successfully carried the university through troubling times. Of all of the areas in the University, the Faculty of Engineering was most affected by these early retirements as so many of its once-young faculty members and staff who had been at Waterloo from the late 50s and early 60s were eligible for SERP benefits. Many of them had skills which allowed them to enter directly into the marketplace beyond the university. With them went the memory of the early years, since so many had been at Waterloo almost from the

beginning. The original strategy praised by Ted Batke and Doug Wright of recruiting many young engineering professors now resulted in a large cohort of professors able to take the early retirement package. Although the Faculty of Engineering worried about the loss of so many colleagues who had been at Waterloo so long, they also recognized that when the University's funding was restored, Engineering at Waterloo was in a privileged position to rebuild ahead of other competing universities.

For the next Dean, Sujeet Chaudhuri, the excitement of Waterloo's founding years began all over again. His primary goals became the recruitment of new faculty members, establishing a new direction for engineering and reinstating its research agenda. Chaudhuri was also successful in bringing major research grants to the university and in mentoring a host of new faculty members. When he retired in 2003, the new Dean of Engineering, Adel Sedra, came to Waterloo from a distinguished career in Electrical Engineering and a seven-year term as the University of Toronto's Vice President, Provost, and Chief Academic Officer. Restless, innovative, energetic, and charismatic, Sedra set out to achieve international recognition for Engineering at Waterloo, to find ways to make it the premier Engineering school in Canada, and to have it counted among the leading Engineering schools in North America. Quite simply, he said, his goal in "coming to Waterloo is to help make Engineering one of the top schools in the world."[59] He also confided that at the University of Toronto they had always envied the place that Engineering had at Waterloo, and on the eve of the university's sixth decade, Adel Sedra's quest seemed within his grasp.[60]

NO LONGER NECESSARY TO WRITE BEER ON THE WATER TOWER

It was no longer necessary to write the word BEER in bold letters on the water tower or to wear a distinctive engineering jacket to make either Waterloo's Engineering program or Co-operative education well known. With more than 11,000 students in work assignments in all of Canada's provinces and in placements worldwide, Waterloo's is the largest postsecondary Co-operative program in the world. Following the original inspiration of President Hagey, Co-operative education at Waterloo is an integral part of each of Waterloo's six faculties. It is also in the process of major changes in the spirit of renewal and innovation. As the University approached its 50th anniversary, many realized that this was also a "tipping point" not just in the Engineering Faculty, but also with regard to Co-operative education which had played such a major part in the success of its program. There were still those who could remember the hesitant days when Co-op was tentatively discussed, and others doubted that it would succeed as a form of education; technical training perhaps, but not education in the classical sense. How wrong they were. Although not for every student, and not for every career, the program of Co-operative education developed at Waterloo was one of the most significant contributions to postsecondary education in Canada in the twentieth century. At Waterloo, however, nothing was taken for granted and the renewal of Co-operative education is part of the mandate for the 50th anniversary.

On the cusp of these changes, and after a forty-one year career with the University of Waterloo – first in the registrar's office, then as Director of Distance Education and eleven years as the Director of Co-operative Education and Career Services – Bruce Lumsden announced his retirement. Like Bill Lennox in Engineering, Lumsden was a student during the tumultuous years of the University's founding, and after graduating from the University of Western Ontario had returned to play a formative role in the creation of this new university. As did the first Director of Co-ordination and Placement, Bert Barber, the new Executive Director of Co-operative Education and Career Services, Peggy Jarvie, is from outside of the university. Her experience was in business, coming to Waterloo from Clarica, now Sun Life, one of Waterloo's earliest Co-op employers. Adel Sedra and Peggy Jarvie saw in the University of Waterloo the possibility of renewing the spirit that had animated it for the last half century; the task is still daunting, but with the opportunities within reach, the sense of adventure is too great to ignore.

CHAPTER FIVE

Waterloo: continuity and change

When George Dixon, a young research scientist in the field of environmental toxicology agreed to come to the University of Waterloo to give a seminar on his research, he had not expected to find employment as a university professor. The type of applied science in which he was engaged was not common at most universities. To his surprise and delight, he discovered that at Waterloo, applied science was looked upon with favour, and he explained, "They valued the applied science that I did."[1] Many scientists at Waterloo, although pure research scientists, had important applications for their work, including former Deans of Science Bob Farvolden and John Thompson. In his turn, George Dixon became Dean of Science, and in 2007 the University's Vice President, Research. Early in 1961, the first Dean of Science, W.A.E. McBryde, recognized that a combination of pure and applied research was important to the success of the University of Waterloo since so many students were in engineering, and for them the application of scientific research was of obvious interest. These students, as well as many in the Faculty of Science, came to Waterloo to take part in its Co-op programs and they hoped to find industrial jobs upon graduation. In a later interview, McBryde explained to Waterloo's founding president, Gerald Hagey, that "at Waterloo we have been an important resource for the chemical industry in this country. Lots of industrial people make no bones of that fact. They look to Waterloo as a source of young men/women who have acquired a chemical education, but also hands-on experience at the industrial level. Their summer jobs haven't been lugging tourist bags around, they have been on the job, and they know how to look at a chemical plant and understand the relationships."[2]

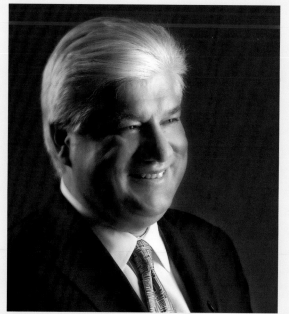

McBryde, however, also recalled that one of his greatest achievements as Waterloo's first Dean of Science was to develop biology and geology as strong research areas, acknowledging that a majority of Science students were committed to pure scientific research and were not in fact in the Co-operative program. McBryde also took great pride in travelling to England and successfully recruiting Noel Hynes, a world-class research scholar at the University of Liverpool who built up biology as a powerful department that was seen as on a par with mathematics and engineering at Waterloo.[3] Hynes's interests in ecology and the environment gave Waterloo a unique perspective which coincided with the research and teaching interests in the Department of Geology of Bob Farvolden in groundwater, ultimately drawing scholars from around the world to Waterloo's Groundwater Institute and to the University's extensive research programs in the Science Faculty.

In 1999, with a personal foundational grant of $100 million and significant contributions from two of his business colleagues and from the municipal, provincial and federal governments, philanthropist and business leader Mike Lazaridis fulfilled a long-held dream of creating an independent world-class research institute in theoretical physics. Although the Perimeter Institute for Theoretical Physics is independent of the University, the opportunity for enrichment of physics programs and the attraction of international scholars to the community has a profound impact on it, and cross appointments between the University and the Perimeter Institute have benefited both institutions. This unparalleled donation was followed by a major gift to the University when Lazaridis and his wife, Ophelia, donated $50 million to establish an Institute for Quantum Computing on the university campus, to advance fundamental experimental and theoretical knowledge in relevant areas of Engineering, Mathematics, and Science and to enhance the developments in the field of Quantum Computation and Information Processing. On Wednesday, January 10, 2007 Amit Chakma, the University's Vice-President, Academic and Provost initiated the University's 50th Anniversary celebrations with the announcement that Nobel Prize winner Sir Anthony Leggett had joined the faculty of the University of Waterloo, further strengthening the University's growing reputation as a world leader in quantum information science. "Leggett's decision to come to Waterloo speaks volumes about the University's rising prominence in the field," said Chakma who had encouraged Leggett to consider coming to Waterloo. On Chakma's invitation, Leggett visited Waterloo in the summer of 2006 and was impressed by the way researchers in pure mathematics, applied mathematics, physics and engineering came together to work in quantum information. The culture and environment is particularly stimulating, Leggett remarked, saying that the Institute for Quantum Computing has, "assembled an outstanding cluster of computer scientists, mathematicians and theoretical and experimental physicists, all sharing a common language. The Institute for Quantum Computing at the University of Waterloo has already become an international leader in the exploding field of quantum information."[4]

The study of science moved far beyond what Dean McBryde imagined when he came to set up shop in a perfunctory lab in the still-uncompleted Physics and Mathematics building. As he reminded President Hagey, "My first vision of the University was in January (1960) and at that time, the only building that was fully up and going was the original Chemistry/Chemical Engineering Building. ... The [now] Physics Building was partly built...but there were still parts of it under construction."[5] Nearly fifty years later, the campus is still under construction with the Quantum-Nano Centre sited for the Commons between the Biology and Chemistry complex and the Mathematics and Computer Building.

In 1981, when George Dixon was offered a position at the University of Waterloo he felt that Waterloo "was perhaps more willing than other universities to accept change and innovation. Its Faculty of Science brought a balanced view that stretched from recognizing the importance of pure research to seeing areas of applied scientific research."[6] Co-operative education helped to support the mentality at Waterloo, where an acceptance of things that could be applied was not seen as a risk, but as a natural evolution and an extension of the University's extensive interaction with industry and government.[7] Waterloo also came of age as

a university when society was making different demands on universities, and the times were perhaps as important as the philosophy of Co-operative education in shaping the direction the university followed. In some ways, the two were indistinguishable.

The Faculty of Science always attracted students who are interested in using science as a preparation for the professions as much as students who are interested in the Co-operative program and industrial careers. This is not surprising, for by its very nature the study of science deals with fundamental questions and the Faculty of Science is also one of the University's most research-intensive faculties in the areas of pure as distinguished from applied research. But then, as the Lazaridis's donations have demonstrated, pure and applied scientific research, each in their separate spheres, offer boundless opportunities.

The Faculty of Science is also home to two of the University of Waterloo's professional schools. The School of Pharmacy, which will admit its first students in 2008 and the School of Optometry which joined the University in 1967[8]. The evolution of the profession of optometry began in 1920 under a Board of Examiners of Optometry. The creation of an independent College of Optometry of Canada in 1925, with some instruction given at the University of Toronto, evolved by 1937 to a three-year course, and its name was amended to the College of Optometry of Ontario. In the post-war years the College trained a large number of veterans who had been involved in medical service overseas and it also began to integrate into its program the range of new knowledge that had come from the scientific and technical revolution arising out of the war years. As early as 1958, President Hagey contacted the College of Optometrists to gauge their interest in a relationship with the soon-to-be established University of Waterloo. Hagey's initiative arose out of a "casual conversation" between Dean Bruce Kelley and Dean E.J. Fisher of the College of Optometry. Four years later when Justice Emmett Hall

163

recommended in his Royal Commission on Health that Optometry be brought within the university system, the University of Waterloo was a natural choice. Interestingly, Dr. W.J. Dunlop, a former Chairman of the Board of Examiners in Optometry, who as Minister of Education had done so much to support the University of Waterloo in its formative years, suggested to President Hagey that the College of Optometry was an appropriate addition to Waterloo.[9] With financial support from the Government, a joint University-Optometry Committee was struck to evaluate the place of Optometry as a discipline within the University and the ability and willingness of the Faculty of Science at Waterloo to develop it as an academic university program. After approval by the University Senate and the Department of University Affairs, Canada's only English-speaking School of Optometry was opened at the University of Waterloo on July 1, 1967, coinciding with the tenth anniversary of the University and the 100th anniversary of the nation.

Like so many others within the University, the first faculty members of the School of Optometry were forced to share laboratory facilities with their colleagues in the Faculty of Science. The School was located off-campus in the former 1911 Waterloo post office building, an historical landmark designed under the influence of the famous Ottawa architect Thomas Fuller. Its King Street location made the clinic readily accessible to the community. Although temporarily displaced in February 1969 by a spectacular fire in the third floor of the post office building, the School flourished at Waterloo, establishing both a research program and a tradition of outreach to the community. Optometry was brought onto the campus in 1974 when the Optometry Building was opened on the North Campus as the first university facility to take its place on the extended campus.

Under the directorship of Jake Sivak from 1984-1990 and again from 1993-1998, the School of Optometry developed a strong research profile in the field of vision science. Sivak consciously changed the School's direction, recruiting international research scholars as well as expanding interdisciplinary research inside the university with cross appointments in Physics, Chemistry, and Biology. New areas such as the Waterloo Institute for Health Informatics, research chairs in Vision Science and In Vitro Ophthalmic Toxicology, and the Centre for Sight Enhancement added to the School's scientific outreach, while another faculty member, John Flanagan, received a cross appointment and research directorship at the Department of Ophthalmology in the Faculty of Medicine at the University of Toronto. Waterloo also developed an internationally recognized centre for research in Optometry and Contact Lenses, while Optometry itself was now recognized by the medical research council as a listed profession and would soon become part of the University's new Medical Sciences Complex on its Kitchener campus.

In 2005, in association with the University of Toronto, the University of Waterloo announced an innovative arrangement by which a School of Pharmacy would be established on a new central site in nearby Kitchener.[10] In no small part, the reputation and direction of Waterloo's Faculty of Science had made this initiative possible. As early as 1985, the Science Faculty had identified an area of expansion with a biomedical focus to build on the strengths of the existing professoriate.[11] Not only did the existing School of Optometry work well within the science faculty, but strong medicinal-chemistry groups and research scholars in biology had an interest in plant products and pharmaceuticals as well as in toxicology. An initiative by the City of Kitchener, including a donation of land and a financial commitment of more than $30 million, strongly encouraged by President David Johnston and the Vice-President, Academic and Provost Amit Chakma, with the support from the University of Toronto, allowed the Dean of Science and his faculty to take the lead and to move the Health Sciences Campus from an idea to an agreement.

Almost immediately following this, the Ontario Government's dramatic decision to create four new branches of existing medical schools and to locate one of them in Kitchener created an unparalleled opportunity for the University of Waterloo. Supported by Mayor Carl Zehr and the members of Kitchener's council who had committed land and funding for the School of Pharmacy, and with the additional commitment of Waterloo Regional Government and its Chair, Ken Seiling, the University of Waterloo struck an agreement with McMaster University in Hamilton to locate a regional campus of McMaster's Michael G. DeGroote Medical School on the University of Waterloo's Health Sciences campus in Kitchener. Regional Chair Ken Seiling explained that the level of municipal government support set a precedent in an area of funding in which municipalities had been hesitant to engage, and he conceded, "This is one of the biggest things that has happened to this community in a long, long time because health care is at the top of everyone's list."[12] Mayor Carl Zehr, whose vision and determination had led the campaign for the School of Pharmacy and the DeGroote medical school, said quite simply that "this was a ten out of ten!"[13] For its part, the University of Waterloo's innovative commitment to move off its traditional campus foresaw that this opportunity to create a unique Health Sciences Campus in Kitchener would also enable it to draw on its strengths to provide an attractive venue for a wide range of health professionals, including those in its leading-edge Applied Health Sciences and Engineering Faculties, as well as in the Faculties of Arts and Environmental Studies. Waterloo's existing programs in health technology, bio-informatics, biosciences, population studies, and biomedical engineering were among the best in the province and the University could also build on its Local Health Integrated Network and its research into Public Health. This is a university that has always seen its relationship with the community as different from the Town and Gown image that has symbolized the sometimes tense relationship between other universities and their communities.

The precedent for the Health Sciences Campus had in no small part been made possible by the University's landmark decision in 2003 to move its School of Architecture from its cramped and outdated quarters on the Waterloo campus to a century-old factory building on the banks of the Grand River in the historic Galt section of the nearby City of Cambridge. Unlike the Health Sciences Campus, which came together over a matter of months, the inspiration and negotiations for the Cambridge Campus for the School of Architecture evolved over several years. Architecture School Director Rick Haldenby once likened the process of establishing the School of Architecture in Cambridge to having twenty-five needles all standing in a row with the eyes of the needles perfectly aligned so that one could thread through them as if it was a single needle. "How likely do you think this would be," he asked?[14] Like so many other events that shaped the future of the University of Waterloo and that set it on a path that differed from more traditional universities, this one, too, is worth telling. Without the success of the School of Architecture in Cambridge, the Health Sciences Campus might never have happened.

In 1967 the province of Ontario, disillusioned with the direction of the architecture program at other universities and anxious to create a new school of architecture to meet the needs of the province's expanding economy, turned to the University of Waterloo where the success of Waterloo's Co-operative engineering program had impressed them. As part of its success in winning the design competition for Expo 67, the Faculty of Engineering's Institute of Design had petitioned the province for the creation of a Fine Arts program in Engineering and although this was not supported, the idea of a program in architecture received the province's blessing.

Waterloo's original proposal for the program in architectural studies to be in the Faculty of Engineering and "housed" within the Department of Design was not consonant with the province's determination to have architecture as a professional school separate from engineering. Many within the University also agreed that the new program in architecture should be broader than engineering and should be university-based.[15] Ralph Krueger, Chairman of the Department of Geography and Planning, in the midst of his own plan to create a new School of Planning

Without the success of the School of Architecture in Cambridge, the Health Sciences Campus might never have happened.

at Waterloo, saw this initiative as a marvellous synergy where the proposed School of Planning and a future School of Architecture, along with interdisciplinary courses from across the university, placed Waterloo in the vanguard of change. Moving forward immediately, the University sought students for admission to a pre-architectural program called Environmental Studies, within the Faculty of Engineering. The concept was to create a School of Environmental Systems Design. What emerged, however, was a new Faculty of Environmental Studies, the first in Canada to offer an undergraduate program in Environmental Studies. This program, then called Man-Environment, had a nomenclature that would soon have to be amended, but one that was entirely appropriate for its time when Canada's national museum in Ottawa was proudly known as the Museum of Man.

The University's Vice-President, Academic, Howard Petch, led in creating the Faculty of Environmental Studies, placing Architecture in it, along with the School of Planning, as an anchor for the new Faculty, which would be built around programs concerned with architecture, planning, and resource development, or "man's interaction with his environment." Petch was frustrated by the almost "robber baron" style of the Dean of Engineering, and at the Senate meeting that approved the new Faculty, he stepped down from the Chair of Senate to push the program through, determined to see Waterloo chart a new course and to broaden its base of excellence. A new School of Architecture and a new Faculty of Environmental Studies were part of the next Waterloo initiative in its expansion as a university.

With limited provision of office space,[16] Architecture acquired class rooms, design space, and faculty offices off-campus at leased industrial space, first at 411 Phillip Street and later at a larger facility at 419 Phillip Street, near the campus, but not part of it. "We became the Phillip St. crowd," recalls Rick Haldenby, a member of an early architecture class and a future Director of the School of Architecture.[17] In buildings that were largely unheated and studios that were improvised space, in this out-of-the-way place on Phillip Street, the School of Architecture developed a culture that pulled together literature, design, drama, and art, and from the beginning the students and faculty began to think in a global context for architectural practice. In a curious way, the physical separation from the campus and the lack of tradition offered a liberating experience that also spoke of the late 1960s and early 1970s. This is not to suggest that there was no contact with the campus, for architecture students rode their bicycles to class for lectures and to the library for assignments, but when classes were over, they returned to Phillip Street where their imaginations were given free reign.

According to Haldenby, "Waterloo's Co-operative program set up a remarkable opportunity from being in school to being dispersed all over the world" which provided a unique instance of connection to global design.[18] In 2005, more than fifty per cent of Co-op placements in architecture were outside of Canada and this trend was present from the beginning. Much of the explanation for the international focus rests with John Hoag, the first Co-op coordinator – whom some regarded as a fearsome figure – who had worked in France, England, the United States, and Canada before taking on the Waterloo portfolio. Hoag saw architecture as international in scope and cultural in its imperative and he stressed this as he found international placements for his students and encouraged them to accede to the challenge that architecture offered. By leaving campus and "camping out" on Phillip Street, the School of Architecture developed on its own and created a unique environment. When, in 1982, the School was relocated for the first time onto the university campus in the infamous orange brick-clad Environmental Studies II building, the separate identity and core values of the school were already established, and for the next twenty-two years Architecture continued to march to the beat of its own drummer. The orientation of its building, with an entrance that faced away from the campus and a largely unused public space between Environmental Studies, the Humanities Building, and the neighbouring Psychology, Anthropology, and Sociology Building encouraged Architecture's more or less happy isolation, while its scheduled off-campus terms in Rome added to the school's international identity.

So successful was Waterloo's School of Architecture that its classes were too crowded and its design space too small. The School was due for the renewal of its accreditation within the architectural profession and there was some doubt that it could continue its program without a major revision to its facilities. No money, or at least not enough money, was available to do justice to what was clearly a flagship program of the University of Waterloo. Fate intervened as it so often had in the past, but

not in a way that anyone would have predicted. In 1998 at a fundraising luncheon in Toronto, Morden Yolles put the case quite bluntly when he commented, "Don't ask me or anyone else to give money for an addition to that dog of a building [on campus]. Build a new one!"[19]

Unfortunately, given budgetary constraints, there was little likelihood of provincial support for a new university building on this or any other campus. Regardless of how valuable the program, traditional funding for universities was impossible. It was necessary to think completely outside of the box. By chance, at a meeting in Cambridge where Haldenby was speaking about urban design and urban renewal, Cambridge businessman Jim Cassel suggested in an offhand remark that "All your problems will be solved if you just move the School to Cambridge."[20] The City of Cambridge was especially anxious to revitalize its historic [Galt] city centre and the interests of the two were tailor-made for each other.

The City of Cambridge was created in 1973 by an amalgamation of several separate communities, including the City of Galt, the towns of Hespeler and Preston, the village of Blair, and parts of North Dumfries and Waterloo townships as part of the overall strategy of the Ontario government to replace the older nineteenth century legacy of county government with a twentieth century prescription of regional governments. The city had been struggling to find its way. Divided from the northern half of the Regional Municipality of Waterloo by the Macdonald-Cartier Freeway (Highway 401), Cambridge sought its identity in the new political reality and resented its loss of prestige and dominance in the southern part of the region. The northern section, predominantly Mennonite and Germanic in its historical origins, retained little in the way of its historical architecture. The mid-nineteenth century, however, had been a prosperous time for the village of Galt, and its buildings reflect an outstanding sense of style, grace, and proportion, providing an impressive example of the well-designed unity of a nineteenth century Ontario business street. Cambridge has one of Ontario's finest examples of pre-Confederation granite building streetscapes. Its major business block, a legacy of ashlar granite buildings, retains much of its 19th century commercial architecture.

Despite the less than attractive urban development along Hespeler Road, with its strip malls and urban sprawl – a sampler of the delights of affluence – the citizens of Cambridge realized if they retained a greater sense of the past, a richer future for their city could be possible. With historic house and driving tours, publications, and education campaigns accompanied by persistent lobbying, Cambridge demonstrated the economic and cultural benefits of living in a community that had retained a sense of its past. However, more was needed to revitalize the community. Arising from this determination to aid their community, a number of leading Cambridge citizens and politicians agreed to raise the necessary funds and to coordinate federal, provincial, and municipal grants to encourage the School of Architecture to consider relocating to the City of Cambridge. The project was supported not only by a consortium of Cambridge business leaders, but also by the Chancellor of the University of Waterloo, Valentine O'Donovan, a Cambridge resident. O'Donovan and his wife Sheila contributed their enthusiasm for the University and $3 million to the project, bringing together the interests of the City of Cambridge with those of the "high tech" University of Waterloo. O'Donovan's company, ComDev, was a world leader in satellite communications, and he and Sheila lived in a classic Victorian home overlooking historic Galt, and for many this personalized the potential of the project.

In retrospect, it all seems so simple. But then, in retrospect most things do. The first suggestion for a School of Architecture in Cambridge was made in 1999. In the following year, Haldenby made a presentation to the Cambridge Chamber of Commerce. Meetings followed in 2000 and 2001. The idea of moving so far from the university campus in Waterloo led some to worry about the impact on the students. The Faculty of Environmental Studies had to be convinced; so did its students. Then there was the University Senate, the Board of Governors' Committee on Buildings and Properties, and the Board of Governors itself. Rick Haldenby became a kind of modern-day music man, leading the parade, passionate in his belief in the benefits to the School of Architecture and insightful in its advantages to the community. As one of the "Phillip Street Crowd," he knew that this could be made to work. A major donation of $2.5 million from the Musagetes Foundation to establish a library in the School to house one of Canada's most outstanding collections of rare books on architecture and design ultimately minimized the anxiety about academic support for the project.

In March 2001, the University of Waterloo, the City of Cambridge, and the Cambridge Consortium signed a letter of intent to follow up on the possibility of establishing a School of Architecture in Cambridge. Negotiations continued with the city, with the university, and with the provincial government, but something went terribly wrong when it was discovered that the cost of remediation of the coal tar contamination on the proposed site overlooking the Park Hill dam was prohibitively expensive. In the time that was available and within the budget that had been proposed, a school of architecture could not be built. It nearly ended there as a sense of discouragement descended over the project. The estimated cost on this site was $35 million. This was clearly impossible and even if it had been feasible, time was running out. With strong support from the City of Cambridge and the consortium of private donors, a solution might still be found. The School of Architecture had already begun to admit students for its new graduate program and the project could not be delayed.

Fate intervened again with the proposal that a former textile mill on the opposite side of the Grand River was available. The mill stood near the picturesque, arched Main Street Bridge, itself an historic landmark, and abutted Queen's Square, where the King's Arms hotel was built in 1835. As the fateful year of 2001 came to an end, the Melville Street property known as Riverside Silk became the preferred option for the School. University leaders and the City of Cambridge had to be persuaded that the Melville Street property could be converted into a world-class school of architecture. Provincial and federal money had to be renewed for this site. The building itself had to be examined and carefully evaluated. In the meantime, academic priorities continued apace, with the first Master's thesis defence scheduled for December 2001. By May

of 2002, it had all come together; the funding, the plans and the students. Known as the "Miracle on Melville Street party," on June 13, 2002 more than one thousand people gathered to celebrate the plans for the School of Architecture. Still, it was not over. With a funding shortfall, the University of Waterloo still decided to move forward, believing this was in the best interests of the university, its students, and the local community. The doors opened on September 7 to receive the first-year class, and the first lecture took place on September 13. When, on Friday, October 22, 2004, the official opening of the school was celebrated, the $27.2 million price was deemed to be exceptional value. Supported by the Regional Municipality of Waterloo, the City of Cambridge, provincial and federal governments, as well as a consortium of local business leaders and several private benefactors, the School of Architecture underlined its commitment to the University of Waterloo.

In an interesting footnote, President David Johnston happily recalled that without the support of the businessmen in what was then known as South Waterloo, the Co-operative education program so important to the success of the University of Waterloo might never have happened. The provincial Director of Education, J.G. Althouse, had included in his budget in 1956 an appropriation for a grant for a trade school in South Waterloo. He suggested that if the South Waterloo group was willing, this money could be reallocated to the not-yet- established Associate Faculties, which became the University of Waterloo. Percy Hilborn, a Preston businessman, took Althouse's proposal to "the South Waterloo people" who agreed to support the development in Waterloo, "even if it meant delaying the procurement of a trade school for them."[21] The opening of the School of Architecture, President Johnston quipped, was long overdue. In a further ironic twist of fate, in 2006 the School of Architecture rejoined the Faculty of Engineering in a process of reorganization within the university.

If the first engineering students nostalgically remember their days in the temporary buildings nestled in a parking lot on the Waterloo College campus, and the students in the School of Architecture recall the camaraderie of the days on Phillip Street, members in the Faculty of Applied Health Sciences may have a more difficult time telling unbelieving students they had offices and taught classes in Seagram Stadium, while others, such as former AHS Dean Bob Norman, shared office space in the basement of Waterloo Town Square, a nearby shopping centre that opened in 1962. Roger Mannell, a future Dean of Applied Health Sciences, first saw the campus as a high school visitor in 1964, and he remembers it as an exciting sea of mud still under construction. When he returned to Waterloo in 1979 from Acadia University's nineteenth century ambience and ivy-covered buildings, he found that Waterloo had dramatically changed, where rolling hills and fully grown trees had appeared as if by magic. Still, his office was not yet on campus, for many professors in AHS were located in a former warehouse on the now famous Phillip Street where the School of Architecture was still located. This was a far cry from the research facilities of the Faculty of Applied Health Sciences' buildings on the South Campus, with state-of-the-art laboratories. Here, Canada Research Chairs conduct major research projects that cut across several disciplines, a Master's of Public Health charts Canada's response to future pandemic outbreaks, and the interRAI Area Network of Canada, led by John Hirdes, is part of a 29-country collaboration gathering health care data and where Richard Hughston's research in cardiorespiratory and vascular dynamics resulted in him serving as a consultant to NASA studying movement in outer space.

FROM 10BX TO NASA

The story of Applied Health Sciences' move from the gymnasium at Seagram Stadium and the basement of Waterloo Town Square to state-of-the-art university research facilities reflects the dramatic growth and acceptance of Applied Health Sciences, from its origins as a one-year Bachelor of Physical Education program in the 1960s to a modern research-intensive faculty in the University of Waterloo. More simply put, from 10BX, the fitness program which Norman Ashton wrote

while in Ottawa at Canadian Armed Forces Headquarters, to Richard Hughston's consultations with NASA, from the almost ubiquitous exercise regimen of the Canadian Government to the frontier of outer space, faculty members in Applied Health Sciences have played a role.

Like so many other universities in the 1960s, the University of Waterloo responded to the dramatic need for high school teachers by introducing a one-year program in physical education. In the beginning it followed the standard Ontario curriculum, but almost as soon as it was established, the program succumbed to the Waterloo mantra of not simply doing better what the others were already doing, but of doing what the others were not doing and setting a new course. The result was the introduction of the first program in Kinesiology in North America.

The Kinesiology program was the genius of Norman Ashton, who came to Waterloo from the Royal Canadian Air Force where he had been the "Physical Fitness Specialist" required to evaluate the effects of physical fitness, fatigue reduction, and alertness of flight crews over extended durations as well as the physical strength required to deal with flight situations where hydraulic systems had failed. The complexity of these tasks went far beyond the normal expectations of physical education programs and opened up for Ashton the intricacy and importance of the study of human movement.[22] A graduate of McGill University, one of Canada's oldest and most prestigious universities, Ashton felt that Waterloo offered a unique opportunity to test his ideas about the study of movement beyond the normal restrictions of teaching physical education to future high school teachers. Waterloo was "a young university" that "prided itself on its uniqueness" and it might be receptive to "another new idea." The faculty members were also young and eager and some of them at least had less of a vested interest in the previous program. The other advantage was Co-operative education, which made University of Waterloo coordinators available to locate jobs for student work terms, thereby providing an invaluable asset to the fledgling proposal. Finally, Ontario restricted the preparation of teachers to colleges of education, and universities were free to develop their own subject matter and were not bound by pedagogical constraints. As Ashton later recalled, "It seemed to me that the situation was made-to-order to try something new and different; all of the necessary elements seemed to be present."[22]

Ashton proposed a program that would include courses in biochemistry, anatomy, physics, neuro-physiology, physiology, and biomechanics, or at least courses that would later come to have this nomenclature. Not only was this a new program, but it was to be multidisciplinary and required faculty members from a variety of different disciplines to contribute to its success. One of the first recruits, Bob Norman, was asked to create a program in biomechanics. He confided that he knew little about what biomechanics was, but was interested in the opportunity at Waterloo to do something new and different.[24] Ashton joked that the University itself was unsure of the field of biomechanics, and in the university calendar in which the course appeared, "a proof-reader, obviously equally unfamiliar with the term, altered it to read biochemistry."[25] Even at Waterloo, change did not always come easily. Nonetheless, in December 1967, the University Senate approved the program in the study of human physical movement to be called kinesiology. Many of the courses that were proposed did not exist, or existed in a form that was inadequate for the purposes of a university department. Faculty members were recruited, and others who had been at Waterloo a short time were encouraged to attain their PhDs and return. As the program developed, faculty members with training in medicine, engineering, physiology, chemistry, psychology, and sociology joined the department. Recognition of the importance of research was encouraged by Ashton in 1968, when he suggested that faculty members with primary responsibility in kinesiology should not have to assume coaching duties in university sports programs, or if they did, these commitments would be secondary to their faculty appointments. Not everyone agreed with these changes and some colleagues at Waterloo, as well as at other universities that were more closely aligned with older methods of teaching physical education, were critical of this approach.[26]

As the program continued, it also broadened the scientific aspects, moving beyond human action in sports to applications in areas such as workplace and safety, minimizing injuries, and improving productivity. The arrival of Gerry Kenyon in 1970 as Director of the School of Physical Education and Recreation and then as the first Dean of the newly-named Faculty of Human Kinetics and Leisure Studies integrated Leisure Studies as a major multidisciplinary part of the program. This area had been added by Ashton at the behest of the Provincial Government, which sought a program to prepare Community Recreation leaders. As the interests of the new faculty grew and as research directions expanded, in response to the report of the Lalonde Commission on Health Promotion, a department of Health Studies was formed in 1978. This was followed in 1986 when under a new Dean, Ron Marteniuk, a multidisciplinary program in Gerontology was integrated into the Faculty. The research agenda of the faculty continued to evolve, and in 1990, the name of the Faculty was changed to the Faculty of Applied Health Sciences.

The appropriation of the word "science" aroused the concern of some in the Science Faculty about the application of science done outside of their discipline, although for those who could recall, as early as 1970 the Science Faculty Council had agreed that the Department of Kinesiology could offer a Bachelor of Science degree. Others in the Department of Recreation were more concerned about the use of the development of "health" as a major theme in the Faculty's orientation. At the same time, others wondered about the "social science" done in the Department of Recreation and Leisure Studies. Their concerns were put to rest by the assurance that leisure studies is a discipline much in demand by biomedical researchers and that researchers in the department have research and citation records that place the department in the top rank in its field in North America, while agencies such as the Canadian Cancer Society and the American Center for Disease Control in Atlanta consult with Waterloo's scholars in the area of disease prevention and wellness.[27] The foresight of Ron Marteniuk, who orchestrated tours and visits to demonstrate not only the quality of the science conducted in the Faculty, but also state-of-the-art laboratories in physiology and biomechanics, carried the day.

What makes the Faculty of Applied Health Sciences unique is the multidisciplinary character of its three main departments: Health Studies and Gerontology, Kinesiology, and Recreation and Leisure Studies. The departments draw from a variety of Applied Health Science Research Groups that range from the Centre for Behavioural Research and Program Evaluation to the Centre of Research Expertise for the Prevention of Work Related Musculoskeletal Disorders and Disability, and from an Ergonomics and Safety Consulting Service, a research area in Population Health Research, to the Murray Alzheimer

Research and Education Program. There is also a Neural Behavioural Assessment and Rehabilitation Program and a UW Research Institute for Aging, as well as the RAI-Health Informatics Project, a $1.67 million research project funded by Health Canada's Health Transition Fund. As in so many other areas, Waterloo's Co-operative education program enabled the university to concentrate on the theoretical research aspects while Waterloo's Applied Health Science students brought from the Co-op terms the practical implementation of many of these ideas.

Recent events such as the outbreak of the SARS epidemic and its pervasive impact on a large scale affirmed the importance of Waterloo's Applied Health Sciences approach, where the importance of health promotion and "health informatics" support and supplement the patient-centred focus of medical schools. The Faculty of Applied Health Sciences is a centre of research and a catalyst for health promotion serving the university and the community in important aspects of health and wellness.

If the Faculty of Applied Health Sciences serves one aspect of community wellness, the four colleges, or University Colleges – St. Jerome's University, Renison College, St. Paul's College and Conrad Grebel University College – contribute in other ways to the strength and integrity of the University of Waterloo. Their sense of community or of "communitas" brought widespread community support and an important physical presence to the rough-and-ready landscape that was the University of Waterloo. Shore and Moffat, the university's first architects, identified a picturesque site for the colleges, explaining that "each faculty, or residence, or church college will form a campus unit of their own, in scale with the buildings and the people using them and will make an important addition to the university."[28] The colleges were situated on land sloping down to the stream on the far side of Laurel Creek where Shore and Moffat suggested that the colleges could develop "similar to the colleges and quadrangles at Oxford and Cambridge Universities."[29]

THE COLLEGES AND THE UNIVERSITY

Conrad Grebel College's first President, J. Winfield Fretz, came to Waterloo as a published scholar with a well-deserved reputation among the Mennonite community in North America. He was an articulate spokesperson for their tradition, and in the era of unrest created by the Vietnamese war, he and the Conrad Grebel community offered an important perspective of tolerance and understanding for these events rather than the intense reactions that occurred at other universities. Winfield Fretz's eye for architecture established the attractive presence of Conrad Grebel College, which was enhanced in 2005 by the addition of a stunning atrium. Dr. Douglas Hall, who inaugurated the presence of the United Church of Canada on Waterloo's campus, is a leading Canadian theologian, one of the most widely read scholars in his field in North America. A.W. Rees, the founding Principal of Renison College, served in Switzerland in the immediate postwar years and later in South Africa, and he brought an urbane insight to university discussions as someone who taught and understood international diplomacy. By all accounts, however, President Hagey's personal friendship and close working relationship with St. Jerome's President, Fr. C.L. (Cork) Siegfried, cemented the important role of the colleges within the University of Waterloo. Without the original and unqualified support of St. Jerome's, Hagey freely admitted that the University of Waterloo may not have had provincial support.

Established in nearby St. Agatha in 1865,[30] St. Jerome's College was an important educational presence in Kitchener and Waterloo. In the years immediately following World War II, it entered into an affiliation agreement by which its students received their degrees from the University of Ottawa. The President of St. Jerome's College, Fr. Michael Weiler, was anxious for St. Jerome's to be part of a Catholic University of Canada centred on the University of Ottawa, and in 1952 St. Jerome's

expanded its academic programs with a $1 million building program in the Kingsdale area of Kitchener. New courses were planned in the experimental sciences, positive psychology, and business administration. All of this was set aside when Fr. Siegfried moved to support the establishment of a new university in Waterloo. Although some criticized his decision, Siegfried stood unequivocally with President Hagey in the movement to be an integral part of the University of Waterloo.

When the idea for a separately incorporated science faculty affiliated with Waterloo College was first discussed by the Cabinet of the Ontario Government, the Minister of Education informed President Hagey that without St. Jerome's support it would not have cabinet approval.[31] Siegfried's determination that St. Jerome's federate with a new university rather than with Waterloo College pushed the university idea forward, and without his insistence, the story of the University of Waterloo would be written very differently. In a letter to C.P. McTague, the Member of the Provincial Parliament who was involved with the establishment of Windsor's Assumption University, Siegfried explained that "St. Jerome's College is prepared to support and actively to encourage any satisfactory plan whereby the two existing colleges (Waterloo College and St. Jerome's College) could cooperate with each other, with any other local body and with the provincial government to improve their educational services. It is the opinion of St. Jerome's College that the most desirable arrangement would be a federation of Waterloo College, St. Jerome's College and a third college under non-denominational control, all sharing a university charter independently of any existing university. If the principle of federation has the approval of the Ontario Department of Education, I am confident that it would receive support from the people of this area."[32] He also explained to Dr. W.J. Dunlop, Ontario's Minister of Education, that "No satisfactory agreement for sharing facilities can be made, unless both colleges operate under the same university charter." "St. Jerome's," he said, "preferred that a university charter be granted to this area simultaneously with the establishment of a non-denominational college, rather than the plan proposed by Waterloo College which would have the new college affiliated with Western University."[33] Siegfried's foresight and the needs of St. Jerome's College led to the creation of a separate, independent university, and Siegfried was a key architect of the federation agreement that shaped the soon-to-be-created University of Waterloo. In light of the ultimate failure of a federation agreement with Waterloo College, the friendship and support of "Cork" Siegfried is all the more important.

Waterloo's four colleges charted a common course in support of the academic goals of the University, while their distinctive academic traditions added breadth of vision and unique specializations. The colleges provide nearly one quarter of all of the undergraduate teaching in the Faculty of Arts in its regular disciplines as well as in stand-alone programs in Social Work, Peace and Conflict Studies, Sexuality, Marriage and Family Studies, and in studies in Personality and Religion, in East Asian studies, and in Music, as well as in outreach specializations to Canada's aboriginal community, to name only some of their areas of interest. St. Jerome's University and Conrad Grebel University College also offer graduate programs at the Master's level. In addition to these extensive programs associated with the Faculty of Arts, St. Jerome's teaches in the Faculty of Mathematics where its courses are oversubscribed and where two St. Jerome's mathematicians hold distinguished research chairs, one in Cryptography and the other in Quantum Computing.

Like the earlier examples of Oxford and Cambridge – or, closer to home, the University of Toronto and the University of Western Ontario – Waterloo's colleges are also residential colleges, and it is here that many of the University's students have their first experience of life on a university campus. Although in recent years the University has dramatically expanded its residence accommodation, the colleges have retained a central position on campus where professors and students co-mingle in a collegial environment. The colleges' outreach programs, including liturgical services that integrate a sense of spirituality with the academic rigour of their programs, offer another dimension to university life. They also bring to the campus an array of prominent musicians and distinguished lecturers in events that are open to the university and the larger community. When added to the diversity of academic and research traditions, the colleges at Waterloo do much to shape the university and its students and will continue to do so in the future.

At the University of Waterloo's fall convocation in October 2006, almost forty years to the day after Ira Needles spoke to the graduating class of 1966, there was a hushed silence when Chancellor Mike Lazaridis approached the dais. This was the University of Waterloo's convocation on the eve of its sixth decade and like those students before Chancellor Needles, and so many thousands since, it was a special moment. Lazaradis's remarks were poignant and touched every student in the room. A former Waterloo student before founding Research In Motion, newly inducted as an Officer of the Order of Canada, and with honorary degrees from the University of Waterloo and the University of Windsor, Lazaridis believed passionately in the importance of education. Taking the concept of "technology transfer" as his theme, he reminded the graduates that the most important transfer of ideas from the university to the world was in themselves. In whatever field or whatever path they chose, the ideas and the values they took with them had the power to change forever the future of this nation, in ways large and small. These were thought provoking ideas from one of Canada's foremost business leaders, who regarded Waterloo's students as among the best in the world. When Bill Gates, the Chairman of Microsoft, came to the University of Waterloo earlier in 2006, he expressed similar comments and reminded Waterloo's students that they were always among those whom his company sought.

Waterloo was never intended to be a university where its students merely did what others had done. From the very first class, the philosophy at Waterloo was to do what others had not done. This legacy was not lost on the other speaker at convocation for the class of 2006, Louise Arbour, who left the Supreme Court of Canada to become High Commissioner for Human Rights at the United Nations, and who told Waterloo's students to take a meaningful measure of their professional lives to protect the "human rights" of people, saying, "We should not let ourselves be intimidated by the size of the challenge." Had the first University of Waterloo president, Joseph Gerald Hagey, been there, he would have been inspired by Louise Arbour's comments, as fifty years earlier, in the face of great odds, he sought support for his ideas for a university that was relevant for its time: a new and untested university with a different philosophy.

The words of Chancellor Lazaridis and Louise Arbour, also rang true for David Johnston, the fifth President of the University of Waterloo. Sitting next to Chancellor Lazaridis at convocation, David Johnston and Mike Lazaridis form an interesting partnership much as Gerald Hagey and Ira Needles did so many years earlier. The differences between Johnston and the first president, Gerald Hagey, are many, but so are the similarities. For David Johnston, university leadership is a form of service. After three terms as Principal of McGill University, moving with his wife Sharon from Montreal's Westmount to a century farm in Heidelberg, Ontario, in the midst of Waterloo's picturesque rural Mennonite hinterland, Johnston accepted the presidency of the University of Waterloo because of the University's innovative character and his belief that he could make a difference to Waterloo's students and to Canada's university tradition.

In the early years of the University, its founding president, Gerald Hagey, was a much sought-after speaker. There was a fascination about the University of Waterloo and Hagey liked to talk about his university and his comments reveal a good deal about the excitement and sense of adventure associated with Waterloo and its students. As he explained to the graduating class at the Ingersoll High School in May 1964, "During the early years of the University our students gained the type of experience that can only be gained at a new University. There were practically no precedents for them to follow; there were no fully organized student societies and there was little, if any, tradition to be found in any part of the university's operation. .... I believe that the students who participated in the organization of the student activities on the campus felt that they were making a major contribution to the development of the University itself and it gave them a sense of feeling part of the University which they could hardly have achieved as easily on an older University campus..."[1] This same spirit, he said, also carried over to the faculty members who, from the very early years, were "conscious of the need to develop excellence at the same time that we were developing new programs. Because of this our faculty members have been encouraged to extend their research work as rapidly as possible. ... What applies to the University in emphasizing the importance of high standards of excellence applies equally as much to each individual. Unless we are prepared as individuals to insist upon our own work being of a high standard, we could hardly expect to achieve a degree of excellence, which will be recognized by our fellow citizens."[2] And as Hagey explained, "Although I naturally feel that the University has made tremendous progress in its first few years of existence, I believe that we have only started. I cannot perceive a time when the universities will not be challenged by new requirements from our society. Equally, I cannot foresee a time when the University of Waterloo will become so hidebound by tradition that it cannot adjust itself to providing education to meet these needs. Already we are trying new approaches and studying others."[3]

WES GRAHAM @ WATERLOO

The arrival in Waterloo in 1959 of a young lecturer in mathematics, James Wesley Graham, symbolized the attitude of the University in ways that foreshadowed major innovations at Waterloo and beyond its campus. A student of Ralph Stanton's in mathematics at the University of Toronto, after graduating with a Master's degree Graham joined IBM, rising to become head of its Applied Science Division. While he enjoyed the excitement of the business world, he disliked its incessant travel and wrote to inquire of Stanton about possible academic positions at Waterloo. Stanton welcomed him, urging Graham's appointment without the mandatory PhD degree, although it was understood that Graham, like so many other young instructors at this stage in their careers, would be granted leave to complete a doctorate, and he and Stanton talked about possible supervisors at the University of Toronto where Graham was already well known. After settling with his family in Waterloo, the following year Graham entered doctoral studies at the University of Toronto, but he became increasingly restless at the interminably slow pace of change, and returned to Waterloo more determined than ever to introduce an educational program that was relevant to the second half of the 20th century. And bring about change he did – and quickly. Wes Graham's imprint on Waterloo and on the development of its international reputation in the area of applied mathematics and computing, would be writ large.

Under his inspiration, instead of restricting computers to faculty members or to graduate students, the University of Waterloo became one of the first universities to make computers available to undergraduate students. This was a revolution that transformed teaching and learning at Waterloo, and later at universities around the world. In 1960, Waterloo began to teach what would be known as computer science courses to undergraduate students in mathematics, science, and engineering. By 1961, IBM proudly announced that its model 1620 computer installed at the University Computing Centre (a room on the second floor of the Physics and Mathematics building), was "available to all the faculties, including engineering, science, and arts. And both graduates and undergraduates are working with the computer."[4] Upon the resignation of Electrical Engineering professor Basil Myers in 1962, Wes Graham was appointed the first Director of the new University Computing Centre, now a separate university department. For this additional responsibility Graham received a stipend of $50 per month. It was probably the wisest investment Waterloo ever made. Graham's leadership after Myers' departure shifted the focus of the Computing Centre from hardware to software and set the destiny of Waterloo on an innovative path.

In October 1964, Graham arranged for the acquisition at Waterloo of the IBM 7040 and IBM 1401 computers, which as an integrated system gave the University of Waterloo one of the most sophisticated hardware packages in North America. Whether this claim was true or not was hard to measure; what is easier to understand is that Waterloo's acclaim placed it in the forefront of a worldwide revolution in the use of computing and Waterloo's undergraduate students took advantage of the availability of Graham's open access policy to claim national headlines. In June 1965, three Waterloo undergraduate students, Gus German, Robert Zarnke, and Hugh Williams solved a mathematical puzzle known as the "Archimedes Cattle Problem" which had first been proposed by the Greek mathematician, Archimedes of Alexandria in 200 BCE. The idea of using computers to resolve this longstanding mathematical problem started over an argument at lunch in Kitchener's Charcoal Steak House, when Williams, a student of number theory, provoked German into trying to prove that it could indeed be solved using a computer.[5] Combining the IBM 7040 and 1620 computers and working only in the evenings when computer time was available, they produced a final solution which had over 200000 digits. The same problem could be solved today in a matter of seconds using Waterloo Maple software, but in 1965 their achievement was published in scholarly journals and in newspapers across Canada.

THE WATFOR COMPILER

Later in the summer, four Waterloo undergraduates, including the ubiquitous Gus German and Bob Zarnke as well as Richard Shirley and Jim Mitchell, wrote the WATFOR compiler for the FORTRAN IV computer language created for the IBM 7040 computer. The compiler was an amazing success and by the fall it had over 2,500 users at UW alone. What was remarkable was that this was done by four undergraduate students working over one summer. By November, five other Canadian universities and eleven universities in the United States were using WATFOR. By June of 1966, two other Canadian locations, thirty-six American, and six others in Great Britain, France, Italy, India, Sweden, and Switzerland had acquired the WATFOR compiler. It increased the 7040's processing speed by something in the order of 100 times, so that a job that had once taken an hour could now be processed in under a minute, and its diagnostic capabilities were superior to most other programs. Users could easily find and correct errors that had been the bane of most previous interpreters or compilers. Essentially, WATFOR made it possible for undergraduates to be able to use computers and to learn from its diagnostic characteristics, thereby dramatically expanding the availability of computing. Its error diagnostic capabilities also drew the attention of senior researchers who immediately seized upon this as well as its speed of operation. Overnight, the name of Waterloo became internationally known among professors and students alike.

Jim Mitchell, one of the four undergraduates who wrote the compiler program, has provided a wonderfully descriptive memoir of his introduction to computing at Waterloo. He came to the university in 1962 to study Chemistry, but was repelled by the odours in the chemistry lab and switched to Physics, and then to Mathematics. From his first encounter with the computer, he was captivated:

About the second month of first year, I was sitting in first year calculus beside Forbes Burkowski, and Forbes had a computer printout of a FORTRAN program. We also took numerical analysis together and I asked him, "What's that?" and he said, "I'm doing the numerical analysis on the computer." We had these old calculators, these mechanical calculators, and we'd go over to the lab and do the iterations, write down numbers, and

solve equations; it was very slow and Forbes had a short program and he showed me how it did one of the problems. He just described to the computer what he wanted to have done. When I asked him how long it took, he said, "Well once I wrote the program, it took about five minutes to do the assignment." I took two hours to do the same assignment, so I was very excited that there was a machine that could do something that was relatively complicated, and so I asked, "How did you get permission to use the computer?" And he said, "Just don't ask" or something like that, because undergraduates weren't really allowed to use computers. (Graduate students and professors had an IBM 1620 at the end of the hall on the second floor of the Physics building.) I found out that I could sneak in there at lunchtime when no one was there, so I went to the bookstore and bought a book on FORTRAN and Forbes taught me some material and within a few days, I was writing my first program and I was just absolutely hooked. This was so much better. So, we started doing this regularly, I'd write all my numerical analysis assignments on the computer. I'd have to copy them by hand onto the things you had to hand in because it would be suspicious to hand in a print-out from the computer...I don't remember exactly when that year, but we began to learn more and more about that machine and it was no longer cool to just write these simple FORTRAN programs, we wanted to start messing with the machine language and the real machine and my first real programming book was Programming the IBM 1620 and it was much more exciting and you could do things at that level that you could not do any other way, including just making the lights go infinitely...By the end of the year, Gus German had learned how to do certain loops so that if you set up an AM radio, it played music because the clock signals were at some frequency and he could cause things to vary in just the right way so that you could play the music pretty loudly. We were doing fun stuff like that. One lunchtime, I was sitting there – I think Forbes was with me, but it might have been Bob Zarnke – and suddenly there was this voice behind me: "What are you boys doing?" It was Wes [Graham] and we said, "We just wanted to learn about the computer" and we had the lights flashing and we were doing things that we weren't supposed to do... We were caught so we basically told him that we had taught ourselves FORTRAN, we had taught ourselves machine programming. Instead of getting mad at us, he started being interested. "What have you got it doing?" I had written a program to start plotting and making curves, because the punch-cards went in and you had this thing coming linearly ... and he basically gave us permission to use the computer at lunchtime.

Graham had seen their passion for computing, along with their obvious talent, and he invited them to stay for the summer doing computer programming. For the next three summers, Jim Mitchell remained at Waterloo writing computer programs, including one that reorganized the operation of the Co-operative education system by linking and then matching student choices for employment with employers' choices of students. It was, he recalled, a simple enough program, based on a combinatorics course that he had been taking in the Mathematics department, and it made possible the rapid expansion of the Co-operative system to additional employers and ensured the match for job placements between students and employers. This innovation set the Waterloo system apart from other Co-op universities and it contributed significantly to the successful growth of Waterloo's flagship program. It also linked Co-op to computing in a way that branded Waterloo's innovative applications to practical solutions and foreshadowed an endless series of computer applications created at Waterloo and applied in the larger community.

Of all of the events of these early years, the development of the WATFOR compiler has become enshrined in Waterloo legend. It begins with Gus German's acquisition of a FORGO interpreter from the University of Wisconsin. Although some have used the word "pirated" to explain the FORGO's arrival at Waterloo, Wes Graham quickly asked for and received permission for its use. The frustrating experience of working with FORGO, however, led Mitchell to propose to Peter Shantz, a young instructor in Mathematics, the writing of a Waterloo version, not as an interpreter, but as a compiler. That summer Mitchell, Zarnke, Shirley, and German took over a classroom in the Physics and Mathematics building and succeeded against all odds in completing an assignment which most of their professors thought was impossible. (Years later, Graham reminded Mitchell that they each earned $1,250 for their summer's work.) Graham held the reins on student enthusiasm, tempered with occasional digressions, and decided that it would be interesting to demonstrate the compiler at IBM's Toronto office. Graham and his four students were greeted with a combination of scepticism and hostility. They were met with an attitude that questioned: Who were these undergraduates? What did they know about computing? A set of test programs the students had made was fed into IBM's own compiler. Mitchell recalls that, "...there

was sort of a tick and nothing would happen for a few minutes and then something would print out and it would tick and then IBM said, 'Okay, that's ours' ... it's working pretty well. Then they ran our compiler on the same tape and it went drrrrrrrrrrrrr as fast as it could go and the stuff was spewing out on the printer, at a great rate and the others just stood there for a moment dumfounded, before looking up and saying almost immediately, 'This could sell a lot of machines to universities.'"[6] Sell a lot of machines, it did.

The 7040 was only the beginning. IBM's new 360 series of machines was more flexible and at least twenty times faster than the previous 7040 and the model 1401. The 360 became the standard for use in universities worldwide, and Waterloo was there ahead of the others. In anticipation of the arrival of a 360 model 75 on campus, Graham and two young staff members, along with a group of talented undergraduates working in the computing centre, created a version of the WATFOR compiler for the IBM 360.[7] Written primarily by Paul Dirksen and Paul Cress, this compiler became the international standard for the most popular scientific computer language of its generation. First known simply as the WATFOR compiler for the 360 and WATFIV when the FORTRAN language extensions were added, it increased the performance of the IBM 360 to the point where it could compile and execute a 45-card job in under 10 seconds, while comparable IBM programs took 13 minutes to execute the same job. Dirksen and Cress were awarded the Grace Murray Hopper Award in 1972 for significant achievements in Computer Science by those under thirty-five years of age.[8] With the distribution of the WATFOR compilers, the name of Waterloo was synonymous with leading-edge computer applications worldwide. The textbook, WATFOR, FORTRAN IV WITH WATFOR, written by Dirksen, Cress, and Graham, published by Prentice Hall, sold more than 250,000 copies at universities around the world and more than 500,000 students used it as a textbook.[9]

The excitement about computing at the University of Waterloo was enhanced in 1965 when Computer Science Days were initiated, bringing thousands of students, their teachers, and often their parents to the University. In 1967 alone, more than 4,000 high school students from 200 different schools visited the campus. The advanced error diagnostics provided by WATFOR allowed students to learn basic programming techniques in less than an hour, and before leaving the university each of them had an opportunity to write a program and to run it on the computer. The opening of the Mathematics and Computer Building in 1967 with its spectacular Red Room and two-storey gallery overlooking the massive IBM 360/75 computer, twenty times faster than the earlier 7040 and 1401, made the University of Waterloo a tourist attraction to anyone visiting the city.

As well as a spirit of adventure and a fascination with the potential of computing, Wes Graham brought to Waterloo business acumen and an entrepreneurial spirit honed while working at IBM. If he could not change the colour of the Red Room, he did not lose his belief that computers should be as simple to use as a pencil and paper, and equally accessible to students and faculty members across the university and beyond. Under his leadership, Waterloo's emphasis on the development of software, rather than building new computing hardware as so many other leading universities were attempting to do, along with the creation of a separate Faculty of Mathematics and its embrace of Co-operative education, continued the University of Waterloo's reputation for practical innovation.

Even before Computer Science was generally recognized as an area of academic specialization, in 1965, Ralph Stanton established a Department of Computer Science at Waterloo. First chaired by Donald Cowan, followed by Pat Fischer and then by John Brzozowski, the department attracted such prominent researchers as Janos Aczel and Alan George, the latter becoming Dean of Mathematics as well as Vice-President, Academic and Provost. Their arrival, along with other scholars in this field, signalled the development of a theoretical orientation to the study of computer science. In 1977, led by John Brzozowski, the Department hosted the Conference on Theoretical Computer Science, attracting research from international leaders in the field. With the introduction of a new curriculum to formalize and standardize the theoretical and mathematical foundations of computer science, Waterloo was exceptionally well placed to maintain its prominent position in the field as well as in the other areas of Mathematics. As early as 1968, one year after the

"We've got to figure out a way to share this technology, but we want to do it so that we don't lose control of it..."

Faculty of Mathematics was created, students from Waterloo placed second in the prestigious William Lowell Putnam Mathematical Competition administered by the Mathematical Association of America. Waterloo's continuing record of successes in the Putnam and in The International Competition for Computer Programming, sponsored by the Association for Computing Machinery and written by students worldwide, is outstanding. In the decade since 1995, combining the rankings in the two competitions, Waterloo's students stood first, ahead of those from all other universities.[10] As part of this evolution, David R. Cheriton, who had earned both his Master's degree and PhD in Computer Science from Waterloo, donated $25 million to his alma mater in 2005 to establish an endowment to fund research chairs, faculty fellowships, and graduate scholarship in Computer Science. His donation was intended to ensure that leading-edge research will continue at Waterloo and to make it possible to attract exceptional students from around the world to Waterloo's programs.

A UNIQUE LICENSING AGREEMENT

An initiative by Wes Graham relating to the distribution and licensing arrangements for the WATFOR compilers also resulted in a policy relating to the ownership of intellectual policy that made possible the creation of several of the University's most influential "spin-off" companies, including WATCOM, WATERLOO MAPLE, and OPEN TEXT. Graham's original intention was to share the WATFOR compiler with other universities and their students, and he made a copy of the first compiler available without charge to anyone who asked for it, so long as they provided a tape on which it might be copied. When difficulties occurred with running the compiler, which in the beginning sometimes happened, Waterloo provided corrected versions. In order to hire students to test and debug the programs and then to send the corrections to those who were registered, Graham decided to ask for a $500 one-time fee. Additional revenue from this was retained by the Computing Centre to engage in further research as well as to distribute the software. Subsequently he charged a $500 annual fee, which users happily paid. Overnight, this established a large revenue stream and a way to deal with this was needed immediately by a university that had no precedent as to how to proceed:

"Our phone was ringing off the hook," Graham's colleague in the computing centre, Peter Sprung, recalled, "And Wes called me and said, We've got to figure out a way to share this technology, but we want to do it so that we don't lose control of it…we don't want to impede the university's reputation because somebody takes our compiler and uses it for the wrong thing."[11] One of the problems was that intellectual property for computer software was not commonly recognized, nor was it easy to patent these ideas. Sprung was despatched to meet with the university's local solicitor, Stewart Mank. According to Sprung, "…We drew up a license agreement that set out the terms under which others could use our compiler. And, while we were at it we decided that we could also charge an annual fee for using the compiler, and we could restrict what they could do with it. … And that license agreement really stood the test of time."[12]

One other critical aspect of software licensing was the ownership of intellectual property, as distinct from the patenting of intellectual property which was being developed by the Faculty of Engineering, for which there also was no formal university policy. As Sprung explained,

"On Wes Graham's advice, a new policy provided that at Waterloo, if you are a professor and if you write software or create any technology as a result of your research or your academic work, you own the intellectual property rights to it, not the university. Since the research was conducted on university-supplied facilities, professors were asked to grant the university a paid up non-exclusive license to use their work on campus for further teaching and research. Other than that, commercial rights were retained by the professors.[13] According to Sprung, "The advantages of this were many. The effect was that if you were a professor or a leader of a research group and if you wrote a program that had some commercial potential and you were interested in pursuing it, you had an incentive to do so because you had control; you owned the intellectual property, it's yours…. We also developed a mechanism within the university whereby if you own intellectual property rights to your software and if you want the University of Waterloo to help you license this on a limited agreement, the

licensing officer would draw up a license agreement that says that you are transferring this right to the University of Waterloo. And then we will use it to license it to other universities like Toronto or Queen's or MIT, or whatever, and get it more rigorously tested before you decide whether to take it to a commercial level. The University of Waterloo was a legitimate licensor for specific kinds of software, but if the individual professor wished to go ahead and set up his or her company, he or she was free to do so. And when they wished the University of Waterloo to stop being a licensor, they would simply inform the university and cancel the agreement. In this system, professors and the creators of the technology retained control. In order to offset costs, 20% of the fees from licensing agreements were retained by the University for overhead, but 80% of the revenue was returned to the research funds of the individual group. Individual professors could assign this to their own research accounts."[14] It all seemed simple enough and a perfectly reasonable set of policies, but it was not done this way in other universities or in other businesses where the institutions, rather than professors, retained ownership of the intellectual property. The licensing of this technology broadly and inexpensively not only generated significant royalties, but it also made the name of Waterloo known worldwide by generations of students and scholars. Waterloo's separately developed patent policy, which, like the licensing agreement, allowed professors to retain the ownership of intellectual property, created an environment in which professors developed initiatives that serve the university and the community, advancing knowledge and moving it from the academic halls to the market place.

The creation of a Computer Systems Group in 1973 separated software development from the theoretical and academic programs of the Department of Computer Science and enabled both units to develop freely in compatible, but very different directions. The Computer Systems Group continued to build on the successes of the WATFOR compilers to become an independent software distribution business within the university, with profits invested in applied computer research at the university. Now free to create a separate marketing division for software products, some members of the Computer Systems Group moved to an off-campus building on Phillip Street known colloquially as the "Bank," which housed a small branch of the Bank of Montreal. The "Bank" was an incubator or hothouse out of which grew an impressive

array of new software and publications, ultimately leading to the creation of WATCOM, the University's first major spin off company. At the same time, members of the Computer Systems Group such as Wes Graham and Paul Dirksen continued to advance computing services on campus, Graham as Dean of Computing and Dirksen as Director of the Computing Centre.[15] Quite separately, computer research continued at a breakneck pace within the Department of Computer Science, where a new Honeywell Computer enabled Waterloo's mathematicians to work directly with colleagues in other major North American universities and enabled Honeywell, which described itself as "the other computer company," to publicize its relationship with the University of Waterloo.[16]

Software development at Waterloo, which first began with the original WATFOR compilers, which were upgraded as each new IBM series of computers was implemented, continued with new business-related software such as WATBOL and WIDGET. This led to a series of adaptations on new computers such as the Commodore Pet, as well as to systems that networked computers which were advantageous in other universities as well as in business applications. This resulted in a relationship between the University of Waterloo and such major computer companies as Digital Equipment (DEC), Commodore, and IBM giving rise to new business initiatives and university procedures to allocate equipment and research funds. In the 1982-83 academic year, Hewlett-Packard announced a computer partnership with UW that gave the university $1.25 million worth of computer equipment. In 1983, IBM announced a $17.5 million research and development agreement with the University of Waterloo. In the following year, Degital Equipment Corporation (DEC) provided equipment worth more than $25 million. The IBM partnership included $5 million for the purchase of 120 PCs and $5 million over five years for research funding. As part of UW's agreement with IBM, the university received three IBM 4341-M02 computers, twenty-four IBM 3350 disk drives, five IBM Series /1 computers, one hundred and twenty IBM Personal Computers, eighty-eight IBM 3277 Terminals, eight IBM 3279 Terminals, four IBM 3272 Control Units, and an IBM 3274 Control Unit.

The complexity of the task to "computerize" the full Oxford dictionary, which in its original form had taken fifty years to complete, was a major undertaking.

Delivery of this equipment was scheduled to take place through 1983 and 1984. These donations expanded Waterloo's emphasis on computing and included exposure to graphics and colour, the networking of computing services into students' residences, homes, correspondence course centres, and co-operative students' work sites, as well as in research for the application of Waterloo's computer methodology to office environments in such areas as image processing, pattern recognition, graphics, and voice synthesis. IBM and the other computing companies saw Waterloo as an important innovator in the ongoing adaptation of computers to education. One spokesperson claimed that Waterloo produced one quarter of Canada's computer science graduates and cited the university's reputation for excellence as the reason for the research partnership between the institutions.[17]

THE INSTITUTE FOR COMPUTER RESEARCH

In 1982, Waterloo's newly-appointed President, Douglas Wright, suggested the establishment of an Institute for Computer Research, under the direction of Computer Science professor Eric Manning,[18] to bring together the wide range of groups interested in computer research. The Institute aimed at enhancing communication and collaboration among the various groups on campus as well as at strengthening external industrial ties. Wright had also persuaded the Ontario Government to support the establishment of the William G. Davis Centre for Computer Research, a landmark building on the Waterloo campus. Naming this building in honour of former Premier William Davis recognized Davis's extensive contributions to the development of Ontario's universities, but more especially his groundbreaking decision in 1966 to provide the funding for the major computer installed in the original Mathematics and Computer Building as part of the capital expense of the building. Wes Graham had suggested to Davis, with whom he had been a class mate at the University of Toronto, that, as this was a Mathematics and Computer Building, the computer could be properly identified as "furnishings for the building."[19] Davis's decision, which was immediately challenged by other Ontario universities, was an important factor in the development of Waterloo's reputation as a school renowned for its expertise in computing. So as not to serve as a precedent for other universities to use this method of purchasing their computers, the funding for Waterloo's computer was amortized separately from the cost of the building, but the computer remained and Waterloo's reputation never looked back.[20]

If it was Wes Graham's friendship with Bill Davis that made possible the acquisition of the IBM 360/75, it was Douglas Wright's friendship with Mike Brookes, who had done so much to shape the design of Waterloo's campus in the 1960s, that made possible one of the University of Waterloo's most telling achievements of the 1980s. As the University of Waterloo pressed ever forward in developing computing applications, Oxford University Press had come to the realization that its venerable and highly acclaimed dictionary was nearing the end of its life cycle, unless it could be reorganized and published in some way using computer-designed technology. As it happened, in addition to numeric computation, researchers at Waterloo were working on new kinds of textual computing, still with databases, but with textual databases rather than numerical ones.[21] It is doubtful that Mike Brookes, who had left Waterloo in 1964 to become Estates Manager at Oxford University, was aware of the intricacies of all of this, but when he learned that the Oxford University Press was considering a computerized data project for its dictionary, he immediately thought of the University of Waterloo.[22]

No one at the Oxford University Press really understood what was involved in making the changes to the production of the dictionary. Brookes, however, mentioned Waterloo's abilities in computing to Richard Charkin, the OUP Head of Reference Publishing, and he also wrote immediately to Douglas Wright suggesting that he contact Charkin. Never one to stand idly by, Wright sent Brookes a telegram outlining the equipment, publication record, and computer capabilities of Waterloo. As he explained to Brookes, the University of Waterloo had quite extensive computing facilities, including a very sophisticated IBM VM installation (based on three 4341's), a large Honeywell mainframe, and several DECVAX's. And Wright added, "there are a substantial number of people on the campus who have considerable experience and expertise with the computer handling of text materials, from inputting, formatting, and editing to online typesetting using our digitized photo typesetter. A number of dictionaries and concordances have been produced in the Arts Faculty," he continued, "and Waterloo had a good deal of experience in providing camera ready copy for book and periodical production."[23] As Wright anticipated, Brookes showed the telegram to Richard Charkin, who immediately suggested to Wright that, "…we would like to discuss some form of collaboration with Waterloo – perhaps on the software development side."[24] Although he was buoyed by the prospects of an arrangement with Oxford, Wright was also pragmatic, warning that "notwithstanding [Richard] Charkin's encouraging tone there would have to be a fair bit of competency to deal with some of these needs [i.e. the technical requirements to OUP] in Britain, and chauvinism is bound to rear its head. There would have to be some pretty good reasons for them to come to us."[25] As it turned out, there were indeed "some pretty good reasons" to come to Waterloo.

The complexity of the task to "computerize" the full Oxford dictionary, which in its original form had taken fifty years to complete, was a major undertaking. Supplements to the dictionary had fallen hopelessly behind since the original publication, and if not brought into the modern age, the dictionary would soon be obsolete. Everyone agreed, however, that it was a priceless asset. Wright extended Waterloo's involvement by personally travelling to Oxford along with the inveterate Wes Graham to assure the Press of Waterloo's capability to take on the dictionary project. He also provided letters of introduction for Dr. Jack Gray from the Department of English and Dr. John Stubbs, a Waterloo historian, graduate of St. Catherine's College at Oxford, and the Associate Dean of Arts, Special Programs. Stubbs and Gray saw tremendous advantages for research opportunities in the Humanities if the dictionary project were to come to Waterloo, and they, too, travelled to Oxford to make the University's case.

Thirteen agencies were invited to compete for the Oxford University Press English Dictionary project, with Waterloo as the only university invited. Negotiations continued throughout 1983; then, on May 15,

1984, Wright and Graham were back in England to announce the University of Waterloo-Oxford University Press partnership. Graham's presence was more than symbolic. His ability to explain the advantages to Oxford of working with the University of Waterloo and his understanding of Waterloo's licensing agreements made possible a relationship from which both parties benefited.[26] Waterloo's reputation in the field of Computer Science was enhanced by being chosen for the prestigious project, while the Faculty of Arts became a leading participant in devising the needs and interests of scholars in the research for which the dictionary would be used in the future. This was Waterloo at its best: curiosity-driven research applied in sophisticated and practical applications. As it happened, this was also the mantra of Douglas Wright as he strove to position Waterloo amongst the best of the universities in Canada and abroad.

The two principal professors in Computer Science dedicated to the project, Frank Tompa and Gaston Gonnet, were not immediately available to begin work on it as both had ongoing research commitments, and while confident that the dictionary project was manageable, neither thought that significant new research in the area of computer science would be derived from it.[27] At a cocktail party at Gonnet's home, Gonnet pulled Tompa aside to ask, "What are we going to do about the OED?" They agreed that it was important to the university, if not to their own research, and that if their own research would not be set back, they should take it on.[28] Little did they anticipate how profoundly the research and its applications would affect the development of computer science and the use of computers on what would be known as the World Wide Web.

The contrast between a very proper five hundred-year-old English university whose first published book was in 1478 and a university not yet thirty years old when the formal letters of agreement were signed was not lost on the participants. The original structure of the dictionary, begun in 1879 by the great lexicographer James Murray, combined with the genius of Gonnet and Tompa's research, retained the integrity of the scholarly aspects of the dictionary with a modern, searchable data base, and brought it into the twentieth century while the powerful string search technology created for the dictionary propelled Gonnet and Tompa's research onto the World Wide Web,

first with Yahoo and then Netscape. What ultimately emerged from this initiative was the Open Text Corporation, spun off by Tompa and Gonnet from the licensing agreements negotiated by the University with Oxford University Press in 1982. Those licensing agreements retained the intellectual property rights of the underlying software for the University of Waterloo researchers, in accordance with University policy. By 1999, with offices in more than fifteen countries and four million people using Open Text products, the genesis of the original string search software first developed for the Oxford Dictionary continued to be adapted and improved.[29] Three years later, the company had added another one million users, with offices in thirty-one countries and twelve languages. Then, in 2004, Open Text returned to the University of Waterloo campus as a major tenant at its Research and Technology Park. The project had implications and benefits for scholarship, research, technology, and business applications that were not even imagined in 1982.

Open Text is an example of initiative and the application of research in the marketplace, and it is only one of many such stories arising out of the University of Waterloo. The intellectual and innovative university environment that made this possible was part of the Waterloo ethos from the university's beginning; but this is not a book of lists, and in keeping with the Waterloo spirit such a list would be out of date before this book is published. In a way, this is every historian's lament when writing about contemporary history. The past is merely the prologue to what is still to come.

As I write these words, it is New Year's Day, 2007. The University's 50th anniversary year has begun. I have been fretting about what I have been able to include of the university's history, and worrying about what has been omitted. Outside my window I can hear the excited voices of students preparing to begin a new university term as the city and the University of Waterloo come alive with their presence. As I listen to the students' raised voices and high spirits, I am reminded of Chancellor Lazaridis's remarks from the Fall Convocation, that the most important transfer of ideas from within the University is the students themselves. Universities exist for their students. Whether Oxford University's 500 years or Waterloo's 50, it is students who make the university's story compelling. The first

students in July 1957 were very uncertain as to what awaited them. They came from factory jobs and lake freighters; some with high school diplomas, most without. They were an unlikely group. Some were recruited by George Dufault, whose job had been to find companies willing to participate in a new form of education and students willing to join in a bold and untried experiment. Others read about the "Waterloo plan" in their local newspapers or heard about it from high school guidance counsellors. None had any previous experience of university education and most were from small towns and communities scattered throughout Ontario. All sensed that this was going to be an adventure in education. Fifty years later, a continuing adventure in education still awaits Waterloo's students.

Photographs often capture the moment better than any historian's text. When I think of the University of Waterloo, one particular photograph comes to mind and it speaks volumes. Amidst the breakneck pace of developing the curriculum and planning new buildings, a ceremony took place in December 1958, to officially open the first building on the new campus. All of the important dignitaries were there: the Honourable Leslie Frost, Premier of Ontario, Ira Needles, Chairman of the Board of the Associate Faculties, Gerald Hagey, President of Waterloo College Associate Faculties, Reverend Delton J. Glebe, President of the Board of Governors of Waterloo College, Dr. G.E. Hall, President of the University of Western Ontario, and Reverend C. L. Siegfried, President of St. Jerome's College. The photo is of the students standing before the old Schweitzer Farm House, looking on with interest. One can only imagine what they were saying to each other or what they were thinking. But there they are: almost all of the university's students in this one image. It is a small group. Some are taking the moment seriously, others are bemused, some may be bored, others just curious. This is the university as it was then. Not yet the University of Waterloo, still only the Waterloo College Associate Faculties, with a former farm house and one new building nearly completed when the students arrived in September. But the look on their faces says it all. This is their university. They are the University of Waterloo.

An Epilogue and Acknowledgements

The 50th anniversary celebration formally began on January 11, 2007. The announcement by Vice-President, Academic and Provost, Amit Chakma on January 10 that the Nobel Prize laureate Sir Anthony Leggett had joined the Faculty was a precursor to the excitement that overtook the campus the next day. It was a wonderful party, with thousands of students, staff, faculty and retirees swaying to music from the 1950s, reminiscing about the display of historical photographs depicting the university's beginnings, and revelling in a sense of excitement and camaraderie. As I watched, I could not help thinking about all that had happened since 1957 and I was especially pleased that so many of those who had done so much to shape the University had joined in the celebration. In the preparation of this book, I was fortunate to have met many of them and to record their memories. Few historians have this advantage and it undoubtedly influenced the history that I have written.

ACKNOWLEDGEMENTS

In 1972, as a junior lecturer in the Department of history, I was invited to meet the President, Burton Matthews, and the past President, Gerald Hagey. Dr. Hagey was anxious that a record of the early years of the university be retained and its ongoing history recorded. Although I was mesmerized by Dr. Hagey's passion for the university's history, I was more interested in the political careers of Sir John A. Macdonald and Sir Wilfrid Laurier than I was in the history of my own university. What was there to be said about a university that was little more than a decade old? Hagey's initiative, however, bore fruit. A university archives was established and Paul Cornell, a senior University history professor and colleague of President Hagey's, agreed to become the honorary university archivist. The result is an excellent University Archives housed in the Special Collections Department of the Dana Porter Library directed by Susan Mavor. Without Susan's support and that of Jane Britton, the Special Collections Archivist, neither the text nor the photographic images which do so much to bring this history alive would have been possible. I cannot adequately express my gratitude to them and to their staff who have assisted me in countless ways, responding to requests for information, new source material, and research support, doing so with tolerance and forbearance as I asked for just one more file, one more time.

President David Johnston, Provost Amit Chakma, and former presidents Douglas Wright and James Downey bear more than a little responsibility for this book. David Johnston is keenly interested in the history of the University of Waterloo and relished reading every chapter as it was written, urging me to keep writing. Amit Chakma was equally enthusiastic and insisted that there were lessons to be learned from the University's history. Doug Wright participated in several oral history interviews, shared his ideas and knowledge about the university, and pressed me onward when my spirits lagged; Jim Downey was always there with wise counsel and the sense that history mattered. I am grateful for their support. They gave me a completely free hand and did nothing to restrict the text or to influence my interpretation.

The completion of this book also coincides with my nearly forty years of teaching at the University of Waterloo. Students challenge our ideas, provoke discussion, keep us intellectually alive and academically honest. They also keep us young. More than that, over the last several years students in my fourth year seminars and in my graduate classes have shared my enthusiasm for this University's history. They have written research papers on topics ranging from student unrest and student riots in the 1970s, which fascinated them more than me, the impact of the war in Vietnam on Waterloo's students, student life and student sports teams, campus architecture and residence life, the development of academic programs, the place and importance of Co-operative education, the development of computing at Waterloo and the concept of "spin-off" companies from the University. The archival research of several students merits individual recognition. Ross Fair, Cheryl Dietrich, Terence O'Riordan, and Julie Mayrand contributed substantially to the material cited in this book. Terry O'Riordan also provided copies of his extensive research notes relating to the first decade of engineering at Waterloo, and Sharon Jaeger, a former student and now a professional historian, gave permission for me to read the text of her unpublished chapter on engineering from 1967-1977. Harold Alkema worked with me on a separate, but related project, *Unbundling Computing at Waterloo*, funded by the Graham Trust. His careful and painstaking enumeration of Waterloo's computing projects and his research paper, the Oxford Dictionary project, was particularly helpful. Not all of this research can be contained within the covers of a book this size. Their research papers are available in the Special Collections Department of the Dana Porter Library.

In addition to student research papers, the Special Collections Department houses the Oral History Interviews which form much of the background for the interpretation herein. I owe an immeasurable debt to those who agreed to be interviewed and for their candour and camaraderie in the interviews.

Colleagues in the history department at the University of Waterloo and at St. Jerome's University, John English, Patrick Harrigan, Geoffrey Hayes, Whitney Lackenbauer, Wendy Mitchinson, Stephen Bednarski, and Carl Bon Tempo challenged me to see aspects of this University's history differently, sharpening my perspective and sometimes changing my interpretation.

Kieran Bonner, the former Vice President and Academic Dean at St. Jerome's arranged for my release from teaching and Myroslaw Tartaryn, his successor at St. Jerome's, continued this privilege and spared me from rounds of committee work. In the midst of watching over her eighteenth-month-old son Harrison, Jennifer Arthur corrected my unruly text, editing needless words and grammatical solecisms. Bronwyn Roe edited the final text with precision and accuracy. Karalee Clerk pushed the design envelope on this project while Bryn Gladding's eye for extraordinary photographs combined with Jeff Funston's creative instincts to produce a book that captures the sense of Waterloo.

As she always does, my wife Elizabeth forgave my absent-mindedness and our foregone family vacations as the deadline for publication drew near. My daughters, Nicola and Janet, and their partners John Hallman and Willem van Heingingen, have been understanding about the vagaries of the University of Waterloo and its demands on my time. I am especially grateful to them and to Elizabeth for their love and support.

When this project was first announced, three of the members of the "fearsome five" regaled me with their memories of the controversial beginnings of the university. Arthur Cowan was the first, attired in a plaid shirt and hiking boots, almost as if he had just walked in from the fateful trek across the campus in the autumn of 1957. He recalled the first students, their sense of adventure, and the uncertainty of the University's future and he described the exploration of the new campus site and the meeting in the recreation room of his home on Erb Street where the Academic Advisory Committee drafted its famous Memorandum No.1. Next of the "fearsome five" came Ted Batke, with

files and sketches and fascinating new information. It was easy to see him as the wordsmith of that memorandum; Ralph Stanton provided several interviews full of insight and intrigue with a phenomenal memory for people and names and places. Professor Stanton subsequently donated his papers to the University Archives.

Although I had spoken to Dr. Hagey, I did not have a chance to interview him for this history, but he recorded comments from many of the first professors and administrators. These tapes are an historian's delight and a rich source of information, as the conversations reveal as much about him as they do about those whom he interviewed. He had also begun to prepare his memoirs and the text of these candid and honest recollections is available in the archives. Had there been time, he might have might have written more, but he might also have edited his memoirs and they would have been less frank and open than the incomplete ms. that he left to us. Much of Dr. Hagey's correspondence is in the University Archives and it, too, reveals his emotions and feelings in ways that are important to historians. Although this book relies heavily on archival print sources, and they are attested to in the footnotes, oral histories capture a sense of the university in ways that printed historical documents cannot and I have quoted freely from them.

I was fortunate to interview all of the subsequent presidents of the University of Waterloo. One of the most candid was also one of my first interviews. Dr. Howard Petch, Acting President and then President Pro-Tem from 1967-1970, met me at his home in Victoria, British Columbia. Petch came to Waterloo from McMaster to be Vice-President Academic. On the day he arrived, Dr. Hagey casually mentioned that he was going to Toronto for medical tests. The news was not good. He had cancer and needed immediate treatment. At a time when student unrest around the world was at its height, Petch was thrust into the leadership of Waterloo. The interview with him brought back vivid recollections of a university in transition. The challenges of that era are hard to imagine now. A subsequent luncheon meeting with four university presidents, Burt Matthews, Douglas Wright, James Downey, and David Johnston in the President's dining room at St. Jerome's University – the irony of the name was not lost on them – proved invaluable. It was interesting to have them recall the highs and lows of their tenure at the University of Waterloo. It was fortunate, too, for shortly after, Dr. Matthews fell ill and our meeting became a haunting memory.

Many others spoke to me about their memories of Waterloo. Carl Dare, a member of that first Board of Governors who attended the fateful meeting when the decision to move to the larger campus was made, offered an insight into the community's response to the idea of a university in Waterloo. E.M. Brookes returned from Oxford to receive an honorary degree and we spent an afternoon walking the campus, recalling the look of the land and those who shaped the university's beginnings. He talked passionately about the influence of Hideo Sasaki and of Shore and Moffat's early campus design and of the importance of Al Adlington in making it happen. He recalled the meetings on the veranda of the Schweitzer house as he and Dr. Hagey watched the campus unfold before their eyes. In time for the 50th anniversary, he ventured into the attic of his Oxford home to send us files, papers, and photographs. I also spent an afternoon with Al Adlington and another with Al Gordon and one with Bruce Gellatly recalling times past, brave and risky initiatives, and lifelong friendships, and I thank them for their hospitality.

I met many of the students in the first engineering class at Waterloo. Jack Kruuv showed me his university jacket, with a pocket for a slide rule and another for a whisky flask. Paul Koch traveled from Ottawa, bringing with him papers and files and memories.

In researching this book, I had a special interest in the development of Co-operative education and its influence on the University of Waterloo. I was invited to join the Legacy Group, made up of men and women who, over the last half-century, shaped Co-operative education in North America. I am grateful to Bruce Lumsden for the invitation to join this group as well as for his many insights garnered over a forty-one year career at Waterloo, and to the others for their friendship.

Along the way, I also became interested in the development of computing at Waterloo, and in technology transfer and "spin-off companies" that contribute to the reputation for innovation associated with this university. The members of the Graham Trust provided financial support and participated in an extensive series of oral history interviews relating to Wes Graham and computing at the University of Waterloo, especially the development of WATCOM, the university's first spin off company. In addition, Savvas Chamberlain, Keith Geddes, Scott Vanstone, Frank Tompa, Gerry Sullivan, Don Cowan, Jim Welch, Ian McPhee, Paul Dirksen, and Mike Lazaridis, along with many others,

spoke openly of the trials, tribulations and successes in taking their ideas to the marketplace. I know that I have not done justice to this aspect of the University's history, but the process continues to unfold at a speed only those who understand Moore's Law will comprehend, and that, too, is part of the Waterloo story to be told at its 50th anniversary.

It is still possible to sense the excitement of those early years and to drive down Dearborn Street, appropriately renamed University Avenue, and by looking carefully, see the original roadbed that led into the Schweitzer Farm, slightly beyond the University Plaza. The remnants of the lane are still there. One can stand on the veranda of the Schweitzer Farm House and imagine with Gerry Hagey and Mike Brookes how the campus might have looked. The original engineering quadrangle and the room in which the board and senate met as they planned the growth of the university is intact. The profile of the Rod Coutts lecture hall on the far side of the engineering quadrangle was built below grade in order to preserve as much as possible of that first quadrangle. The plaque where Prime Minister John Robarts opened Engineering II and where Dana Porter confided his "fatherly feelings" for the University of Waterloo remains. On the other side of Laurel Creek and "Hagey Pond" are the original four colleges, where the landscape design of Hideo Sasaki is striking. But for the trees, one can still sense the rawness of the rough campus, but only with imagination, for as Sasaki predicted, the landscape creates its own mystical effect on the campus. These are memories of times past, but much of the University of Waterloo's history can be experienced. At the Peter Russell rock garden, it is possible to go further back in history and understand the geomorphology of this area. Those who want a tangible sense of the past can walk to the North Campus and sit on the veranda of the 1856 John Brubacher house, and closing one's eyes for a moment, one can recall the early Mennonite settlement and the farmlands which surrounded the University of Waterloo. Go there and try it. You will see what I mean. Waterloo's campus suggests a university that is oriented to the future, but it is also a place where one can experience its past as a university and while students embrace the next half-century and beyond.

KMM

Waterloo, January, 2007

"The Presidents"

Ken Fryer, David Sprott, Arthur Beaumont, 1967

Mike Brookes at "Hagey Pond"

"Moving Day, 1958"

"Cooper Wrecking to the rescue"

"Waterloo: Here they come!"

"A bad hair day"

Dean Wright greets international students

Moving into Village 2

Pollock and Matthews

Graduation at last!

"Sit In" at the bookstore

A new warrior for the "Warrior's Band"

ACM Programming: 1998 North American Champions

Wes Graham "The Father of Computing at Waterloo"

Kesavan, Myers and Lawson: the IBM1620: "early computing"

Bill Forbes

"The Red Room: A UW Icon" The IBM 360/75

"Exactly how old is this?"

A moment in the sun: at last!

Mathematics: 2nd in the Putnam 1968

"Engineering Rules!"

Televising Waterloo games

A "truck load" of computers from DEC (1984)

Measuring the "mini"

"A Serious Moment: Convocation at Seagram Stadium"

Dana Porter Library: Where are the trees?

Computing Before WATFOR

Chancellor Needles at Convocation

"Student Life at Waterloo"

Bill Davis, Gerry Hagey and Waterloo: A long friendship

The New Oxford English Dictionary

Oxford University Dictionary meets its Waterloo (1984)

David Suzuki and Friends at Waterloo

Jim Downey

Alan Adlington

Bill Tutte

Doug Wright by "his building"

Wes Graham

Jim Welch, Ian McPhee: WATCOM: UW's first spin off company

Unplugging the 740: Matthews, Dirksen and Graham (1980)

"The Campus Centre"

"Water Sports"

Alan George: A Man for All Seasons

"I want to graduate from UW too"

The Two Jims: Jim D.

The Other Jim: Jim K.

A.S. "Bert" Barber

W.A.E. (Pete) McBryde

K.A. MacKirdy

Ira Needles

Mike Brookes

"Solar Power: Let's go UW"

Oh, to be young

Canadian University Women at Waterloo

Douglas Wright's Enthusiasm

Recognizing a President

"The Captain"

Burt Matthew, "Cork" Siegfried and Norm Choate

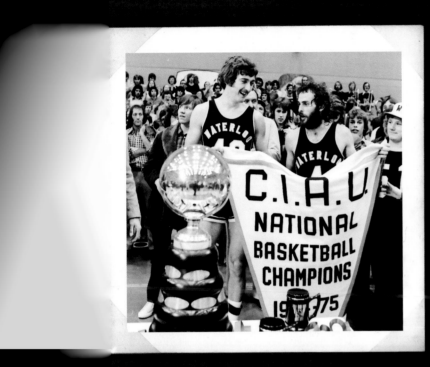

Basketball at Waterloo

Ken Lavigne and Perter Sims

"Building the Library"

Jim Mitchell and Peter Shantz

The Schweitzer House Reborn

Unfurling the "Pink Tie"

Building a University: Truly Mud and Dreams

Tent City: A Shortage of Student Housing

Leaping the hurdles of University Life

Chancellor Pollock

"Mace Bearer"